A MELTZER READER

A MELTZER READER

Selections from the writings of Donald Meltzer

edited by

Meg Harris Williams

with chapter introductions by

Grete Tangen Andersen, Morten Andersen,
Miriam Botbol, Martina Campart, Irene Freeden,
Trond Holm, Renata Li Causi, Neil Maizels,
Robert Oelsner, Tomas Plänkers,
Lennart Ramberg, Kenneth Sanders,
Jon Morgan Stokkeland, Lilian Stokkeland,
Lars Thorgaard, Eirik Tjessem,
Meg Harris Williams

published for

The Harris Meltzer Trust

by

KARNAC

Published in 2010 by Karnac Books Ltd.
118 Finchley Road, London NW3 5HT

Copyright © 2010 The Harris Meltzer Trust
Copyright © 2010 Meg Harris Williams for editorial matter
Copyright © 2010 individual authors for introductions

The rights of Donald Meltzer, Meg Harris Williams, Grete Tangen Andersen, Morten Andersen, Miriam Botbol, Martina Campart, Irene Freeden, Trond Holm, Renata Li Causi, Neil Maizels, Robert Oelsner, Tomas Plänkers, Lennart Ramberg, Kenneth Sanders, Jon Morgan Stokkeland, Lilian Stokkeland, Laars Thorgaard and Eirik Tjessem to be identified as authors of this work have been asserted in accordance with §§ 77 and 78 of the Copyright Design and Patent Act 1988.

All rights reserved. No part of this publication may be reproduced, stored in a retrieval system, or transmitted, in any form or by any means, electronic, mechanical, photocopying, recording, or otherwise, without the prior written permission of the publisher.

British Library Cataloguing in Publication Data
A C.I.P. for this book is available from the British Library

ISBN 978 1 85575 784 4

Edited, designed and produced by The Bourne Studios
www.bournestudios.co.uk

www.harris-meltzer-trust.org.uk
www.karnacbooks.com

CONTENTS

	Contributors	vii
	Foreword by Meg Harris Williams	xi
1	*Psychoanalysis as a human activity* introduced by Kenneth Sanders	1
2	*Dream Life: the generative theatre of meaning* introduced by Miriam Botbol	7
3	*Temperature and distance* introduced by Neil Maizels	21
4	*A psychoanalytical model of the child-in-the-family-in-the-community* introduced by Martina Campart	35
5	*Money-Kyrle's concept of misconception* introduced by Lars Thorgaard and Jon Morgan Stokkeland	45

6	*The delusion of clarity of insight* introduced by Tomas Plänkers	55
7	*Tyranny* introduced by Irene Freeden	69
8	*Dimensionality, adhesive identification, splitting* introduced by Renata Li Causi	81
9	*The impact of Bion's ideas* introduced by Meg Harris Williams	89
10	*Aesthetic conflict* introduced by Lennart Ramberg	103
11	*On Bion's Grid—later thoughts* introduced by Robert Oelsner	113
12	*Sign, symbol and allegory* introduced by Grete Tangen Andersen, Morten Andersen, Trond Holm, Jon Morgan Stokkeland, Lilian Stokkeland, Eirik Tjessem	121
13	*Some personal statements* On his analysis with Melanie Klein; Invention and discovery; The thinking breast; Religion and psychoanalysis; The principles of child psychotherapy training; The nature of supervision; Countertransference and "showing it"; Observation and counterdreaming; Good luck	131
	Meltzer's books and concepts	145
	References	149
	Index	

CONTRIBUTORS

Grete Tangen Andersen is an authorized psychologist and specialist in clinical psychology for child and youth mental healthcare, working at an out-patient unit in Stavanger, Norway.

Morten Andersen is an authorized psychologist and specialist in clinical psychology, at present working for the Norwegian court.

Miriam Botbol is a clinical psychologist and member of the Psychoanalytic Group of Barcelona (GPB). She is the author of books on infant and young child development and co-author of *Psychoanalytic Work with Children and Adults, De un Taller Psicoanalítico*, and *Bebes: Experiencias desde un Vértice Psicoanalítico*. She works in private practice and teaches and supervises in Barcelona.

Martina Campart, PhD, is senior lecturer at the Department of Social Work, Malmo University, where she is responsible for the courses in Psychology and in Reflective Learning in Social Work Education. She is a psychologist with a background in philosophy, focusing on emotional intelligence and uses of narrative in the integration of psychoanalysis and cognitive psychology.

Irene Freeden is a senior member of the British Association of Psychotherapists, a training analyst and supervisor of the British Psychoanalytic Association and a member of the International Psychoanalytic Association. She has been involved in setting up a BAP psychoanalytic training course in Oxford, where she also works in private practice.

Trond Holm is an authorised psychologist and specialist in clinical psychology with a Master's degree in philosophy working at an outpatient unit in Haugesund, Norway.

Renata Li Causi is a psychoanalyst and member of the British Psychoanalytical Society, working in private practice in London.

Neil Maizels is a clinical psychologist and psychoanalytic psychotherapist in Melbourne, Australia. He has a long-standing interest in the arts and literature, and has published many psycho-analytic papers.

Robert Oelsner, MD, FIPA, is a Training and Supervising Analyst of the Buenos Aires Psychoanalytical Association and of the Northwestern Psychoanalytic Society. He is an IPA certified child and adolescent psychoanalyst and is in private practice in Seattle, and teaches in Seattle, San Francisco, Minneapolis and other cities. He is the co-author of *Bion Known/Unknown* and *Melanie Klein in Buenos Aires*, both published in Argentina.

Tomas Plänkers is a Research Scholar at the Sigmund Freud Institute in Frankfurt/Main, specializing in clinical and social psychoanalysis, and also works in private practice. He is a member of the German Psychoanalytical Association and the International Psychoanalytic Association and a training analyst at the Frankfurt Psychoanalytical Institute.

Lennart Ramberg is a training analyst of the Swedish Psychoanalytical Association and a member of the International Psychoanalytical Association and the International Federation of Psychoanalytic Societies. He works in private practice. Most publications are in Swedish; see www.lennartramberg.se.

Kenneth Sanders, formerly a GP, is a Fellow of the British Psychoanalytical Society, and has been a training analyst for the Tavistock Child Psychotherapy Course. He is the author of *Post-Kleinian Psychoanalysis* (Karnac, 2001), and of books on psychoanalysis and the family doctor.

Jon Morgan Stokkeland is consultant psychiatrist at the Division of Psychiatry, Stavanger University Hospital, where he is engaged in educating and supervising psychiatric residents. He is a member of the Norwegian Institute of Psychotherapy, and has published papers on dreams.

Lilian Stokkeland is consultant psychiatrist at Sola Psychiatric Centre, Division of Psychiatry, Stavanger University Hospital. She is a member of the Norwegian Institute of Psychotherapy.

Lars Thorgaard, MD, is consultant psychiatrist and psychotherapist in the National Health Psychiatry in Herning and is in private practice with psychoanalytic psychotherapy and supervision in Århus, Denmark. He is a member of the Danish Society for Psychoanalytic Psychotherapy and former chairman.

Eirik Tjessem is an authorized psychologist and specialist in clinical psychology for child and youth mental healthcare, working at an out-patient unit in Stavanger, Norway.

Meg Harris Williams is an artist and writer with a special interest in aesthetic experience. She collaborated with Donald Meltzer in *The Apprehension of Beauty* and *The Claustrum*. Her latest books on psychoanalysis and poetry are *The Vale of Soulmaking*, *The Aesthetic Development* and *Bion's Dream*. Website www.artlit.info.

FOREWORD

The following selection from the writings of Donald Meltzer is intended to offer new readers a taste of his ideas and teaching. Each chapter consists of a substantial extract from one of his books or papers, and is introduced by one of his colleagues and former students.

Donald Meltzer was born in New York in 1923 and studied medicine at Yale. After practising as a psychiatrist he moved to England to have analysis with Melanie Klein, and for many years was a training analyst with the British society. Meltzer worked with both adults and children. Initially his work with children was supervised by Esther Bick, who was creating a new and influential mode of psychoanalytical training at the Tavistock Clinic, based on mother-child observation and pursuing the implications of Melanie Klein's discoveries in her work with children. Meltzer taught for some years at the Tavistock, where Martha Harris (his third wife) was head of the Child Psychotherapy training course. As a result of their joint travelling and teaching across the globe, this method of psychoanalytic psychotherapy became established in all the principal Italian cities, and in France and Argentina.

Meltzer's ideas and methods were considered controversial by some. He left the British Society as a result of disagreements about methods of teaching and of selection of candidates for psychoanalytical training. Instead he supervised psychoanalytically oriented professionals in atelier-style groups throughout Europe, Scandinavia and South America, whilst continuing to practise privately in Oxford; later his visits also included New York and California. His method was to ask supervisees to present sessions of unedited clinical material, rather than finished papers. He was much loved by his supervisees and several of these, both individuals and groups, have documented their experiences.[i] Since Meltzer's death in 2004 many international conferences have taken place to consolidate and continue his work—in London, Florence, Buenos Aires, Savona, Barcelona, Stavanger, Sao Paulo and Seattle.

Meltzer taught psychoanalytic history and saw himself as following in the tradition of Freud-Abraham-Klein-Bion. Although he was not personally supervised by Bion, he was profoundly influenced by him and was probably the first analyst to describe ways in which Bion's more abstract conceptualisations—particularly from his later work—could find clinical use in the consulting room. He was also however an original theorist in his own right, believing that psychoanalytic "models" of the mind required continual expansion to accommodate new clinical observations, and that the development of model and method were interdependent. Some of his most significant and widely used developments of Kleinian theory include: the "aesthetic conflict" the foundation for normal development, based on the internal mother-baby relationship; "intrusive identification"—a form of projective identification associated with life in the "claustrum" (narcissistic pathology); "pseudo-maturity"—a common clinical manifestation of arrested development; "adhesive identification" and "dismantling" in two-dimensional autistic states; and the "preformed transference", referring to the patient's initial preconceptions about a psychoanalytic relationship which have to be overcome before a genuine transference can be established. He also

---

[i] See for example Cohen and Hahn (eds.) (2000), R. and M. Oelsner (2005).

reappraised the qualities of the "combined object" as discovered by Melanie Klein, stressing its beneficial rather than overwhelming nature as a generator of mental development. This became part of Klein's "theological model" (as he called it). Meltzer made the link between Klein's view of unconscious phantasy as expressing the emotionality of internal family life, and Bion's focus on thinking as a means of containing emergent thoughts. He also made explicit the significance of Bion's revision of Freud's "death instinct" as negative emotionality—that is, as an absence of emotional contact rather than straightforward destructiveness.

Like Bion, Meltzer stressed the need for psychoanalysis to acknowledge its cultural roots and to make constructive links with philosophy, theology and the arts. He had a lifelong passion for the visual arts. In London he met the Kleinian art critic Adrian Stokes and became a member of the Imago Group (which included among others Richard Wollheim, Wilfred Bion, Roger Money-Kyrle, Marion Milner and Ernst Gombrich). With Stokes he wrote a dialogue "Concerning the social basis of art", indicative of his prevailing search for structural links between psychoanalysis and art forms. Later, owing to the influence of Martha Harris's family, his interest in how this may be done expanded from the visual arts into literature. He viewed the relationship between analyst and analysand as an aesthetic process of symbol-making, and this has had an influence on the philosophical perception of the relation between art and psychoanalysis.[i] As Silvia Fano Cassese expresses it, in her *Introduction to the Work of Donald Meltzer*:

> Meltzer's interest constantly turns to that area which is difficult to describe in words and perhaps cannot be expressed in conventional language: the emotional area of non-verbal communication, of reverie and unconscious thinking. (Cassese 2002, p. xvii)

This underlying preoccupation with the aesthetic qualities of psychoanalysis may be seen in most of the extracts in the following collection. There is limited space here for clinical material, but sufficient to introduce to readers the scope and nature of Meltzer's

---

[i] See Gosso (2004) and Glover (2009).

contribution, and to suggest the wider social context in which he saw psychoanalysis. He believed it could contribute to nurturing the "lost children of the personality" and thereby the world in general—provided its practitioners could themselves discard its institutional tyrannies and instead, latch on to "the spirit of it".

It seems appropriate to introduce this little book with a quotation from Martha Harris on the subject of psychoanalytic "pioneers", in which she points out the tension between their personal struggles to formulate ideas, and the subsequent reception of those ideas in the world. She is speaking of Freud, Klein and Bion, but what she said in 1978 may appear now—some thirty years later—to be equally applicable to Meltzer:

> The dependent group structure so often manifests itself in the reliance upon a crystallized selection of the theories of Freud (the original Messiah), sometimes pitted against a similar extrapolation from Melanie Klein (a latter day saint). Bion is unlikely to escape the same fate. Their theories in such a climate of polarization are suitably selected and presented to eliminate the essential questioning, contradictions and progressions inherent in the formulations of pioneers who are constantly struggling to conceptualize the clinical observations they are making.
> (Harris 1978, p. 328)

Meltzer was a prolific writer and his books and many papers have been translated into French, Italian, Spanish, German, and some into Portuguese, Japanese, Swedish and Norwegian. Meltzer's books in English are published by The Harris Meltzer Trust, a continuation of the Roland Harris Educational Trust which he and Martha Harris founded in 1970, in association with Karnac Books. A full list of books and papers may be found on the Trust website, www.harris-meltzer-trust.org.uk.

Meg Harris Williams

CHAPTER ONE

Psychoanalysis as a human activity

Introduction by Kenneth Sanders

The *Psycho-Analytical Process* (1967) was Donald Meltzer's first book. He and his colleagues were conscious that Melanie Klein had bequeathed a legacy of work to be done on the phenomenon she called projective identification, an infant's unconscious phantasy of intrusion into the interior of its mother which confuses identities. It was a time of great optimism and even excitement at the prospect of new discoveries and greater potency for psychoanalysis with both children and adults.

Yet the introduction to the book suggests that the term "intrusive identification" may be preferable to "projective identification". It is evident that Meltzer's attention is also on the contemporary publications of Bion which are establishing a form of projective identification that is not intrusive but containing. In a few more years the view of the world seen from the intrusive "paranoid–schizoid" position, in conflict with the "depressive" position from the non-intrusive type of identification, will come to be seen as the essence of the analytic process, in which intrusions into the mind of the analyst are experienced and recognized as those of an internal child into an internal mother. Then they may be studied, through containment and thought, unconsciously, in the "counter-transference" of the analyst.

The book describes a five stage process which Meltzer regarded as having a "natural history": these being the gathering of the transference (differentiated from the "preformed transference"), the sorting of geographical confusions, the sorting of zonal confusions, the threshold of the depressive position, and the weaning process. It is the phenomenon of the transference that I think prompts Meltzer to write as he does in the final chapter, "Psycho-analysis as a Human Activity", about "the serious question how anyone can practice analysis without being damaged?"

The chapter reprinted here discusses what may be done to preserve the analyst's integrity and protect both analyst and analysand from harm. Meltzer suggests that it is necessary for analysts to be in "racehorse condition", without which their work "will neither bear lasting fruit nor achieve conviction in their own minds."

Psychoanalysis as a human activity[i]
(1967)

Freud's early sanguine assumption that anyone who could learn to analyze his own dreams could practise analysis has progressed to its own antipodes. We now must ask the serious question how anyone can practise analysis without being damaged. Of course every occupation has its special hazards, so no complaint is allowable. Rather it is necessary to look with a sober glance at the hazards of psychoanalytic work, construe and test the safety measures and prophylactic schemes.

No doubt in its own way the so-called training analysis has been the bastion of self-defence of the analyst against the rigours of analytic work and will continue to be so, most realistically when

---
[i] Chapter 9 of Meltzer's *The Psychoanalytical Process* (1967), pp. 92-95.

it is continued in a systematic way as a self-analysis. The second rampart has been the analytic method, the faithful pursuit of which has been the psychoanalyst's best defence against being lured into the ambush of counter-transference activities, the harbinger of which is almost always a breach in technique.

Probably neither of these preparatory schemes can continue to function effectively for the practicing analyst without the scientific society of other analysts, at seminars and scientific meetings, supervisions and congresses. The history of analysis in the future is not likely to include the lone pioneer bringing this discipline to new areas of the earth. It will almost certainly be possible only as group efforts. What part the published literature plays in all this is still, I believe, obscure. Certainly only the intellectual outlines of a scientific advance in our field is communicable in writing, except to the rare individual with first-rate literary talent, such as Freud.

Now, I mention all these wellknown aspects of the problem in order to set them aside and focus attention on a more individual and personal level of the predicament: the practice of psychoanalysis as an act of virtuosity, a combination of artistic and athletic activity. Here the term "condition" becomes as applicable to the psychoanalyst as to the race-horse, although its substance needs elucidation. This I think is the term central to this chapter: not the skill, nor the knowledge, nor the character of the psychoanalyst, but his "condition", and how to stay in it, rather than falling out of it.

Just as an athlete's condition has a background in training and a violinist's a background in practice, so an analyst's "condition" has a background in a daily, weekly, term-wise and yearly scheme of activities which are calculated to be in direct and immediate support of his analytic performance. I could name some of the areas which require modulation. For instance: the number of hours of work, the amount of money he earns, the distribution of types and severity of illness in his patients, the amount of rest between patients, the amount of note-writing and note-reading before and after patients, the extent of participation in post-graduate education, the amount of reading of the literature, of writing papers, of lecturing or teaching—of holiday. The list of course could be expanded, but for each item in the supporting structure the analyst must find and maintain an optimum, being prepared to alter it when evidence demands, and to resist its alteration in the face of external demands.

In all such considerations there must be a guiding principle. The aim is stability, the secret is simplicity, but the guiding principle, I suggest, should be "strain", balanced but close to the limit. A colleague reported to me that her son, when chided for his many rugger bruises, replied that "if it didn't hurt it wasn't sport". I have referred to psychoanalytic activity as a mixture of artistic and athletic effort perhaps because of this central fact—that to be done well it must "hurt". It must be done under great strain, approaching the analyst's limit. Only on a background of work-under-balanced-strain can there emerge that mysterious function of creativity, which alone enables a worker to feel he has a place in a scientific fellowship of peers, rather than in a guild of masters, journeymen and apprentices. The problem is a social one as well, for the preservation of scientific individuality and avoidance of enervating isolation is no easy task, where "schools" and "groups" abound. But the social and individual problems are very closely linked, as my list suggests.

The reason that psychoanalytic activity may be placed on a footing with those of the virtuoso and the athlete is because they all rely absolutely, in the heat of the performance, upon the unconscious—rallied and observed by the organ of consciousness. It is fortunate that psychoanalysis tends to impose regularity, although perhaps too few analysts take advantage of this by keeping their schedules in order: the same patient seen at the same time each day, occasional professional activities such as lectures and meetings left for the evening, etc. It is noticeable that the quality of work later during a day is adversely affected when a patient or student cancels, even in advance, leaving a gap in the day's work. Welcome as the relaxation may be, or useful as the time may prove for other activities, it breaks up the "pace" of the work.

When it is recognized how exacting analytic work is, how "off" days can impede the deepening of the transference in the earlier phases and pose obstacles to the working through later on, the need of planning to maintain "pace" and "condition" stands forth clearly. Seeing a patient through the "threshold" into the depressive position at infantile levels of the personality is certainly the crucial step in establishing the basis of mental health, free from psychosis. But penetration through this twilight zone of values in object-relations requires the utmost effort of both patient and analyst. Mere time and repetition will not accomplish the working through. This period, which usually covers at least two years of difficult work, can certainly be ranked with the task of the long-distance runner or mountain climber, and is often so represented in patients' dreams.

I believe that analysts practicing in the Kleinian framework, which centres so much on character analysis and the achievement of integration, will not get through this difficult phase of the work with their patients without sustained "top performance". Without such clinical accomplishment their work will neither bear lasting fruit nor achieve conviction in their own minds. Patients not carried into the depressive position will relapse; scientific findings not bound—to some degree—to manifest and enduring clinical improvement in patients lose their anchorage in humanity and their supporting structure in social value. This may not render them less scientific nor correct, but will seem to their authors to rob them of importance. How long can a person endure in this strenuous work without the support of social accomplishment and scientific achievement? Not long, I think.

What, on the other hand, are the manifestations of the "damage" of which I speak, short of clinical breakdown? The answer is surprisingly simple and distressingly public. Failure of development! It must overtake almost every analyst eventually, for the vitality and concentration required for continued growth are not to be found except in the rare genius—a Freud, a Melanie Klein. Nor is it harmful to the movement for its tired members to fall back into conservative ranks, to become the modulators of exuberance. But it seems fairly clear that others who fall back from negligence or revulsion against the demands of the task become destructive critics and not modulators of progress.

CHAPTER TWO

Dream life:
the generative theatre of meaning

Introduction by Miriam Botbol

Dream Life is one of the books by Meltzer that has most enriched clinical practice, owing to his formulation that dreams are generators of meaning in the analytical relationship. Written after *The Psycho-Analytical Process* and *The Kleinian Development*, it is sown with ideas that he will extend and pursue deeper in future papers and books.

In Part A he revises the theoretical basis of Freudian concepts, distinguishing "a baffling division between his tendency to form and prove rigid theories, and his extraordinary capacity for observation and imaginative speculation" (p.11). The chapter that deals with the expansion of Freud's metapsychology by Klein and Bion is a splendid summary of ideas in *The Kleinian Development*. Two important differences with Freud are spelled out: the dream is a real vital experience, and affects are previous to their representations. At the beginning of Part B Meltzer presents his new theory of dream life: dreaming is thinking; meaning is not captured from external reality, but generated by internal reality. He says: "In writing this I become increasingly aware of the magnitude of the task undertaken in this book and, with that, the impossibility of doing more than laying a groundwork of a new theory of dreams. Clearly I am attempting to formulate an aesthetic theory of dreams" (p.29). Part C examines the practice of dream investigation, the borderland between thought and action, and the difference between dream exploration and dream analysis. Meltzer writes: "I feel certain that the exploration is the more important, the more artistic aspect of the work. The patient's growing identification with the analyst's exploratory method is a far more important basis for his gradual development of self-analytic capacity than any striving towards formulation that he may evince" (p.147).

The book ends with a very original contribution: a method for those who have already been through analysis to supervise their own self-analysis through dreams. In contrast to Freud, for whom dreams are limited to the working through of previous psychic material, for Meltzer "where an analysis has set growth in motion once again, this growth goes on in the quiet chrysalis of dream-life" (p.177).

Dream life: the generative theatre of meaning[i]
(1984)

We have come some distance in examining the historical basis for a new theory of dreams, the epistemological problem concerning the evidence of dream-life, the grounds for considering dreaming as a form of unconscious thinking equivalent to the actions and play of babies and small children, a theory of symbolism which places it at the core of the process for thinking about the meaning of our emotional experiences, and finally an outline of the theory of extended metapsychology upon whose foundation we wish to construct our theory of dreams. It is necessary now to outline the theory itself so that we may examine its various components in some greater detail.

---
[i] Chapter 6 of Meltzer's *Dream Life* (1984), pp. 86-95.

Let us start with some dream material to which we may refer back as we go along. You will recall the four "crucifixion" dreams:[i] the cleared bridleway, but for the hazel saplings; the young couple worshipping their tomato plant; the inhibited necrophilia; and the paralysis by Mr Parker 51. Let us add to that series another duet of dreams from a young man who returned to analysis after a weekend reporting that he had a new girlfriend who seemed very interested in him, had gone back to his flat with him but had probably been disappointed that he had made no sexual advance to her. The trouble had been that he had not yet written the lecture which he had to deliver the morning of the session to his senior colleagues, although he had known of it for over a month. Not only had he disappointed the girl but he had had to cancel the lecture to his students as well. Two little dream images were vivid in his mind from the brief nap he had had in his office after writing until five in the morning:

1. Richard Nixon, although not yet elected President, seemed to have been given full use of the White House and its facilities, which he proceeded to abuse to set up his gang.

2. Mr Callaghan, who was visiting Washington on a state visit with his family, had not even had a car put at his disposal, but all were being squeezed into a taxi.

The first patient's dreams appear to reveal something of the infantile conflicts that underlie various aspects of his adult life and his approach to the termination of the analysis: the country walker and naturalist; the religious man with mystical trends; the sexual man and his sensual greed; the creative man and his writing inhibition. In all four dreams he is keenly involved in emotional conflict. But the second patient is distanced as an observer of a

---

i From the previous chapter: a man in his forties, approaching the Easter break, dreams 1) a newly-cleared bridleway has nonetheless three hazel saplings growing in the middle; 2) a handsome young couple are kneeling in a manger before a young tomato plant with two branches and a tomato at the end of each, sprouting from a Gro-bag; 3) in the anatomy lab his woman analyst shows him a female torso with which he wishes to have intercourse but cannot bring himself to do it; 4) he is lying on a bed when a tall thin man of 51 enters and lies across him; he is paralysed, in will, so that he cannot throw him off.

state of affairs in his internal world which has interfered with his pursuing his desires and meeting his obligations; a psychopathic bit of his infantile personality is given free access to the facilities for thought (the White House, representing the breast), while his good internal family is given short shrift. Upon this internal model the apportioning of his waking life-time is determined.

We spend one third to one quarter of our lives asleep and the experiments with rapid eye-movements (REM) demonstrate that at least twenty per cent of that time is occupied with dreaming. People are clearly divided in their attitudes towards sleeping as well as towards dreaming, ranging from those who consider that part of life to be one of the great pleasures, and those who lament the loss of time that could be spent in other waking activities if only some drug could be discovered to obviate this physiological nuisance. If we take seriously Bion's suggestion that the neurophysiological apparatus has evolved a mind which can feel, think, remember, judge, decide, communicate on the basis of a model, that model being the experience of the gastro-intestinal system, it would not surprise us to find that the mind behaves like a ruminant animal. It seeks its food, ingests it and then settles down to ruminate and digest it. This does not seem too fanciful a metaphor, especially if we consider that metaphor is the method par excellence by which the mind operates. Bion has given us a theory of thinking which envisages this ingestion (the emotional experience) and the process of digestion (alpha-function, the Grid, Ps<–>D, container-contained, L, H and K vertices, transformations). But of course, as he stresses, it is a relatively "empty" hypothesis, and he has left us the task of filling it with life, particularly clinical life. We must remember that the gastro-intestinal model has room in it for other possibilities: the evacuation of the indigestible as well as the potentially poisonous byproducts of digestion. If we are to construct a theory of dreams upon this model, it must allow for these three processes: digesting the experiences to make available the truth as the "food of the mind"; evacuation of the indigestible, irrelevant aspects of the emotional experiences; evacuation of the lies which are the "poison of the mind" generated as by-products in the Negative Grid.

Such a theory seems, and indeed in many respects is, very different from Freud's. His view that the latent content has always to be worked upon by distortion to deceive the censorship, finds considerable similarity to the distinction between the truth which dreams struggle with and the lies that invade them to deal with the excesses of mental pain inhabiting the conflicts. And of course there is some truth in the idea that the dream is the guardian of sleep in so far as the excesses of anxiety may indeed disturb the sleeper, just as undue stimulation from inside the body or from the environment may do. But we will not wish to assign to this trivial function more than a subsidiary position in our theory. The dreams of our lecturer illustrate the very simple device of distancing by which the conflict and its attendant anxiety may be modulated in the dream process—a device surely "as easy as lying".

In a similar way Freud's idea of the day residue can also be embraced, but we need to look more deeply into the question of the selection of items from the hubbub of daily life which find expression. He noted the surprising fact that the day residues seemed often to be trivial matters, far from the conscious preoccupations and dramas of the day. Rightly he concluded that some particular link to infantile experience was necessary for a daytime event to qualify for dream representation. But that was all formulated in days long before the analytical method took firm hold of the transference as a continuous process whose systematic study could be viewed as the heart of the psychoanalytical method. Today analysts who have preferred this more immediate method to the reconstructive-retrospective one, naturally think of the infantile processes as current, ongoing, uninterrupted by the waking conscious experiences of the day. Rather, the unconscious processes of dealing with the emotional experiences—that is the aspects of experience which bear significance of intimate human relationships, as against the practical matters involving human or non-human objects in the outside world—would indeed appear from analytical experience to form a continuum. Susan Isaacs' "unconscious phantasy" which Melanie Klein exploited so fully and which Bion has assigned the position of Row C in his Grid (dream thought and myth) would seem a suitable concept for the description of dreaming. That is, we would consider dreaming to be as continuous in the mind as is digestion in the body, but concentrated more fully on its task when the other mental processes of dealing with the outside world are in abeyance during sleep. This supposition is strongly borne out in the consulting room by the phenomenon which some patients refer to as "flashes"—sudden inexplicable vivid visual images, seemingly unrelated to the immediate verbal exchange. When they are treated as dream images they yield a rich insight into the infantile transference active at the moment.

The intrusion of these "flashes" into the flow of talk in analysis is reminiscent of what Freud called "the body entering into the conversation"—the classic example being Dora playing with her reticule. Here we would say that the "dreaming process has entered the conversation" and entered it as a visual language, often as poignant as a political cartoonist's drawing worth a thousand words.

And it is this extended concept of language, the diversified language of the multiplicity of symbolic forms (Cassirer, Langer, Wittgenstein, Russell) to which we must turn our attention. If we are to view dreams as a language, we must take it as one that is essentially internal, a mode of internal communication. This means that, as with verbal language, we will need to study and comprehend not only its lexicon but its grammar. I hesitate to say "syntax" for that seems to imply a more minute structuring that the problem of dreams—like that of composition in the graphic arts or music—would seem ready to reveal to us.

But the grammatical structure of dreams—the way in which separate dream passages or images seem to relate logically to one another—often seems to be apparent. For instance, our lecturer's dreams seem to have an "if this… then this" structure. Our Easter patient's series might lend itself to this paraphrase: "As long as A, B and C, it is no wonder that S." As long as I still want to destroy mummy's little saplings because I cannot produce little tomato plants myself, and am tempted to use her body merely to satisfy my sensuality, it is no wonder that my pen lies heavy in my paralyzed hand."

But if we are to approach dreams as internal dramas to whose debates we wish access we must be content to derive a very imperfect understanding of what is happening on the stage, whether it be the stage of our own minds or of our patients. It is not just that the acoustics are poor, as it were, or that the actions move at too rapid and complex a pace, or that we cannot keep track of the vast array of Chekhovian characters; the trouble lies with language itself. Not only are we incapable of a perfect understanding of the meaning of any language, whether it comes from ourselves or another, but no language can capture perfectly the meaning of the inchoate thoughts it seeks to ensnare.

The trouble would appear to lie in two directions: one direction is that the transformation of nascent thought into any language is rife with distortion; the other is that every language has its limit of representability. Even if we could synthesize all the symbolic forms in some super ballet-opera, we would still be left with that residue that Wittgenstein [1922] calls "what cannot be said but must be shown"—the area of emotional intimacy where nothing but the contact of baby-and-breast or lovers embraced can communicate.

Treating dreams as a language is not foreign to Freud's ways of thinking at all, for he compared the analysis of dreams to the translation of a foreign language. But perhaps we would wish to take issue with him about the method involved. His own comparison of the translation of Livy from Latin to German followed the schoolboy method of first making a literal translation and then rearranging the thoughts into literate German. That may be a good enough description of "translation" but it is not the same as "reading Latin". We would wish to "read dreams": in the hope we might aspire in time to learn the dream-language of each of our many patients—but the task appears daunting if not impossible.

In fact it is not the method we use, for we do not have access to the patient's dream in the same sense that we have to our own. Probably many analysts do follow a "translation" method of working—or at least they think, as Freud thought, that they do so; but experience strongly suggests that this is not what happens. In keeping with Bion's dictum of "resisting memory and desire", difficult as this may be in relation to anecdotal material or historical recollection, it comes very easily and naturally when listening to a dream. What seems to happen is that the analyst listens to the patient and watches the image that appears in his imagination. It might cogently be asserted that he allows the patient to evoke a dream in himself. Of course that is his dream and will be formed by the vicissitudes of his own personality. But after all, years of experience on the couch and of subsequent self-analysis might reasonably be expected to have given him a certain virtuosity with the language of his own dreams. From this point of view one might imagine that every attempt to formulate an interpretation of a patient's dream could imply the tacit preamble, "While listening to your dream I had a dream which in my emotional life would mean the following, which I will impart to you in the hope that it will throw some light on the meaning that your dream has for you."

You will recognize that this method does not really correspond to the "intuitionist" one which Freud abjured. Surely there are moments when intuition, even inspired intuition, enters into analytic work and evokes the "funny you should say that" type of response from the patient. And of course we intuit rather than observe the emotional atmosphere in the consulting room as it changes from moment to moment. But I would not wish to stretch the concept of intuition to say that I "intuit" French or Italian, even though it might be that my imperfect language of those languages and my incapacity for fluent thought or speech in their medium cannot match my comprehension when they are spoken slowly.

Perhaps the best link to earlier attitudes toward work with dreams is again Ella Sharpe's [1937] emphasis on "poetic diction" in the dream. But poetic diction is something that we all, not only Bion, consciously aspire to. We would like to be able to talk and write poetically, utilizing all the artistic devices not merely for embellishment but for richer and more precise communication of the emotional meaning that we hope lurks in our unspoken thoughts. We would hope to be able to speak to ourselves and to others in a manner that helped us to discover what we think, perhaps even what we know. And we would join with Prospero in paying respect to our dreams as the fountainhead of this knowledge of ourselves and others. But we must learn the language, to "govern the ventages", in order to have access to this "eloquent music" wherein lies the "heart of mystery" of ourselves.

But poets can be liars as well as prophets, as Plato emphasized, and we cannot look upon dreams as telling the truth, the whole truth and nothing but the truth. In so far as they tell the truth, it is the truth about how emotional experiences are dealt with in the depths of the mind; but truth is not always treasured there, for it is freighted with mental pain. Our lecturer's distance from events in Washington may be the truth about the events but it is not the truth about his distance from them. The image of the Crucifixion may be the truth about the patient's feelings about the coming termination of his analysis in terms of "Father, why hast thou forsaken me?" but it is not the truth about his capacities to struggle against the domination of his infantile greed, envy and jealousy.

Bion has given us a theory which formulates at least three methods of distorting the truth, which he has called Column 2 of the Grid, alpha-function working in reverse, and the Negative Grid. The first method, of alleging something that is known to be false in order to hide our ignorance of the truth, is one with which we are all familiar in clinical work and daily life. It is exemplified by our great penchant for "explaining" by adducing causal relations which we know do not exist: we say "because" when we only mean a temporal series of events. The second method, alpha-function in reverse, can occasionally be identified in dreams, and we can see it in operation in the consulting room when patients make meaningless mincemeat of a not unreasonable interpretation. But the Negative Grid is, I suggest, still terra incognita which work with dreams should help us to map. In this Negative Grid we can expect to find all the devices which have been described as "mechanisms of defence" —the naming of which may help us to locate them in operation but tells us little, epistemologically, about their inner workings.

Since our intention is to construct a psychoanalytical theory of dreams in the spirit of the "extended" metapsychology of Klein and Bion, we must face the complexity of the task. The epistemological aspect we have already argued, but the geographic presents some problems. Not only must we reckon with the division of the mental "world" into its various spaces, but also the lack of unity of the mind. Splitting processes divide one part from another; projective and other modes of narcissistic identification confuse the distinction between self and object; while introjective identification fosters the evolution of the adult part of the personality. The distinction between the dream process and the observation of this process raises the problem which we have metaphorically described as the "theatre for the generating of meaning", and it may prove useful to follow this image in defining the varying roles of different parts of the personality *vis à vis* any particular dream as well as the geographic locality of the dream action.

In these theatrical terms, for instance, there can be little doubt that our crucified fellow is the star of the show in all four dreams while our lecturer is in the audience. We could arrange a table of organization of our theatre, a hierarchy of participation: critic, audience, producer, director, character parts, ingénue, male lead, female lead. Perhaps in the Brechtian spirit we could add "the Gods", descending occasionally to evaluate the progress of these mortal children.

The task would not, at this moment in our scientific history, seem quite so complex with regard to the geography, stage set, the "world" in which the drama is being enacted. These would seem to be restricted to two major possibilities: inside or outside the objects, particularly inside or outside the body of the mother. But we have already begun to learn from the study of confusional states that the world inside the mother's body may be subdivided into distinct, or at least distinguishable, sub-worlds from the point of view of their meaning.

So clearly we are going to employ Bion's "seven servants" [Bion, 1977] in our investigation, remembering always that "why" means "reason" and not "cause" in the mental sphere. Why, for instance, have I omitted from my geographic hit list the area "nowhere" of the delusional system? I wish to exclude it from our theory because I feel, from my experience, that the delusional system is most usefully thought of as generating hallucination rather than dreaming, whether the person is awake or asleep. That is, if we take the delusional system in the sense of a "place" that is located essentially "nowhere", we imply that what goes on there has the meaning, essentially, of "nonsense", a tissue of lies, Pandemonium. It is a mental space where truth is of no interest, where no conflict between truth and lies occurs, where no reality testing—either by multiple vertices of thought, consensual validation of sensa or experimental action—is relevant. The "White House" that Richard Nixon has been allowed to invade may still be the inside of the mother's breast, but once he has organized his gang it may be turned into the delusional system of "Watergate"—paranoia. Once Stanley's glasses have been smashed and his drum destroyed in Pinter's *Birthday Party*, he is ready, mute and confused, to be carted off to "Monty" by Goldberg and McCann. Waking and sleeping have become an irrelevant distinction.

But to return to the personae in our Theatre for the Generating of Meaning: how are we to describe the psychological structural basis of the different roles? If we remember the definition of consciousness as an "organ for the perception of psychic qualities", we can still ask the question, "Which character in our theatre is, at the moment of dreaming, in possession of this organ?" But also, "Is it the same as the recaller and narrator of the dream during the analytical session?" We must allow for the possibility that they may not be—in fact probably usually are not—the same. This theme of distancing from the heart of the emotional conflict would appear to be the most common method of modulating mental pain; or perhaps it would be more correct to say—in order to distinguish "distancing" from "mechanism of defence"—the most common way of modulating contact with the mental pain. The degree of distancing in this sense would allow us to consider Melanie Klein's concept of "denial of psychic reality" on a graduated scale, in keeping with our experience in the consulting room of the gradual approach that patients often make to their pain. It would also add a certain precision and substance to Freud's concept of "working through" which would go beyond the type of process of relinquishment which he spelled out so remarkably in *Mourning and Melancholia*.

Perhaps it has already become apparent that the model of dream-life we are constructing is at great variance with the archaeological model of the mind which is so explicit in Freud's work but still implicit in Klein's. What have we to put in its place? One answer would certainly be "vertices"—different points of view. Our model theatre with its array of participants implies a unity of drama but allows for a great diversity of viewpoint about the drama, as in the great Japanese film *Rashomon*. One can imagine taking a group of children to the theatre and asking them afterwards what the play was about. One little girl would tell about the pretty woman with the beautiful dress, while a little boy would relate the shooting of the villain by the hero. This unity of drama and diversity of viewpoint also provides us with a vantage-point fom which we can observe the basic unity of theme in serial dreams whose outward trappings seem so diverse—what I will call "dream continuity". This type of unity of drama can be both distinguished from and superimposed upon the grammatical type of unity that has already been imputed to the dreams of both our country-walker and lecturer. But dreams that may be brought to a single session do not always come from the same night; and indeed we would wish to have the means of showing the "narrative continuity" of dreams that can be spread over months and years of the psychoanalytical process.

This long process of analysis which Bion has called a "protracted dream" and which he has illustrated in *A Memoir of the Future* is of interest to us not only in itself. We are also concerned with the relationship of these internal dramas to the actions, interests, values, plans and hopes which follow on from the dreaming process. These of course do not come under the heading of "day residue"—the intake from waking life that impinges on the dream-life. What shall we call them? We are already aware from analytical work of the relation of acting out to dreaming—or is it particularly the relation of acting out to the remembering of dreams? But beyond this spill-out of infantile drama, what of the fruitful harvest of those dreams which do succeed in grasping the nettle of mental pain, resolving a conflict, relinquishing an untenable position? We will surely wish our hypothesis about dream-life to shed some light on this question of growth and development of character. We have adopted an unequivocal position in regard to this matter, for after all, in describing dream-life as the "theatre for the generating of meaning", we do clearly imply that the outside world is devoid of meaning until it has been generated and deployed outwards. Studies of autistic children—children with primary object failures, two-dimensionality and adhesive identifications—have given a theoretical and clinical firmness to the objectionable idea that "meaninglessness" can be a significant phenomenon in the lives of human beings.

We cannot contentedly leave this outline of the theory of dream-life without some comment on the momentous importance that certain dreams have in people's lives. Schreber's dream of being a woman in interocuse, the Wolf-man's dream of the wolves in the tree, may illustrate perfectly those haunting dreams which form the nucleus of severe psychopathological developments. But there are dreams, as Emily Bronte said, which "go through one's life like wine through water" [*Wuthering Heights*], enriching one's vision of the world with an intoxication of emotional colouring as never before. Or is it a heady vision that was once apprehended and then lost, awaiting a dream to reinstate its dominion in the aesthetic relation to the world? When such a dream has visited our sleeping soul, how can we ever again doubt that dreams are "events" in our lives? In this dreamworld there is determined the great option between an optimistic and a pessimistic view not only of our own lives, but of Life.

CHAPTER THREE

Temperature and Distance

Introduction by Neil Maizels

This pivotal paper could be considered an experiment in notation. Selecting a session, with a view to analyzing his own technique, Meltzer attempts to find a way to observe and write down the non-lexical aspects of his communications to the patient. This takes on directly what had previously only been framed indistinctly and indirectly in psychoanalytic theory—the issue of tone, distance and "music" that is conveyed and modulated in the analytic interpretation. Meltzer conveys the possibility, and even necessity, of a constantly refreshed self-reflection by the analyst on the internal dynamics underpinning the range of tones intimated in one's interpretative offerings. Whilst this sort of reflective adhocracy is often present in supervisory moments, it had never been taken so fully seriously, on an equal footing with *levels of anxiety* "correctness" in interpretative work.

The paper belongs to the period when Meltzer was beginning to consider more seriously the nature and requirements of psychoanalysis as an art form. This encompasses such problems as crafting a private language, and developing a feel and pitch—through mysterious but ingenious identifications with one's internal guides—for addressing different parts of the patient's self, in the heat of the transference drama. It involves a constant re-sculpting of basic principles of technique into a more flexible resonance of holding-tone, within each session, as the analyst struggles with the limits of mere cleverness or adhesive theoretical adherence. This brings up the interesting question of how much of the psychoanalytic craft is teachable in seminars and lectures and how much can only be imbibed and developed through internal identifications.

The key to the paper (almost in the literal musical sense) is in the italicized remarks accompanying each of Meltzer's interpretations. These self-asides modify the model of the virtuoso analyst. They show us the analytical dreamings which produce the stuff of interpretation, and which lead on to the later "counter-dreaming" model of the analytic field as a collaborative identification with the inspiring-combining internal couple. As such the paper marks a significant stage on the way to the conceptual leap forward of "aesthetic reciprocity" in *The Apprehension of Beauty*.

Temperature and distance as technical dimensions of interpretation[i]
(1976)

The task of supervising others helps one to notice things about one's own clinical work that would otherwise have escaped attention. While this is true about the content of comprehension of material, it seems even more true of technique. Our so-called teaching of technique is a peculiar and ill-defined area—a mixture of basic technical principles, of technical ingenuity within this basic method, of stylistic elements, and even of inconsequential idiosyncrasy. In this paper I wish to try to separate

---
[i] This paper was written in 1976 for an EPA conference in France and first published in A. Hahn (ed.) *Sincerity: Collected Papers of Donald Meltzer* (1994), pp. 374-86.

out this area of the *limits of technical ingenuity within the bounds of fundamental method* in order to pay attention to a particular aspect of it—namely, *ingenuity of verbal expression*.

Before launching into the body of this enquiry, it is necessary to define the boundaries of this area of technique as distinguished from the other three. The basic technical principles I employ are those derived from Freud and Melanie Klein, modified by my own view of the method as process. In this view the analyst's task is to create a setting in which a systematic evolution of a transference process may evolve, be monitored, and be assisted by interpretation. The distinction from Freud's method of investigation of the transference as resistance and in the service of reconstruction is clearly defined. Thus *interpretation proper* as a metapsychological statement (with genetic, dynamic, structural and economic aspects of the transference defined) can be distinguished from more *general interpretative exploration* of the patient's material, which is intended to facilitate its emergence.

This basic method lends itself to rich variation by ingenuity and can be distinguished fairly clearly from technical experimentation. Similarly, the area of ingenuity can be distinguished from those elements of style that are emanations of the analyst's personality, in the social sense. These stylistic modulations, insofar as they are observed by the analyst himself, are presumably allowed to continue because he deems them of no special significance for the work in hand, and he would therefore not consider them valuable for formulation and communication to students. They are, however, just the elements in his way of working that will be mirrored and perhaps caricatured by his own analysands insofar as their identification processes remain narcissistic.

Finally, by an "area of inconsequential idiosyncrasy" I mean to distinguish that area of an analyst's behaviour with a patient that is dictated by his adaptation to the peculiarities that are not part of the psychopathology of the patient. These might include assisting a handicapped patient, special politeness to women, simplification of language for foreigners, etc.

To return now to the area of "technical ingenuity" within the limits of basic technique. I wish to define it more precisely in terms of its internal structure and its significance for the method, and then to go on to examine the particular segment of it that is the main subject of this paper: temperature and distance as dimensions of verbal ingenuity. Some years ago I became aware through my work with children and with very ill adult patients that I felt very restricted by concepts of timing on the one hand, and on the other hand, by Melanie Klein's precept of seeking out the deepest anxieties implied in the immediate material. I was aware that this latter applied mainly to her method for what she called "establishing the analytic situation"; but it was also, in my opinion, characteristic of her approach in general. Both these approaches, and perhaps the possibility of their being mutually exclusive, were felt to be restraints upon spontaneity of communication and eventually of thought. The former carried a bad conscience towards the patient of reserve bordering on secrecy, and invited omniscience in the analyst. The latter was felt to hamper free exploration of the material, and gave a tone of explanation to the proceedings that belied this more uncertain and exploratory monitoring of a process in the patient. I felt that it encouraged an element of passivity in the patient's dependence, and an unrealistic responsibility for control in the analyst.

In contrast, I found that I wished to find ways of expressing my peregrinating thought in order to share it with the patient but without leading him, without causing alarm, erotic excitement, or confusion. Insofar as the aim was to encourage enrichment of the material in order for unconscious intuitive processes in patient and analyst alike to function more widely, this was felt to be a useful preparation for the patient's introjection into his internal objects of analytic qualities of mind in view of the hope of his becoming capable of self-analysis in the future, when rectified personality structure would make this a real possibility.

I also noticed that this wish was finding implementation in a linguistic differentiation between a language of uncertain rumination for expressing exploratory thought (interpretive activity) and one of commitment for presenting metapsychological statements (interpretation proper). When I examined this development in my technique more closely, I could see that I was employing verbal techniques for achieving these aims that might reasonably be called modulations of temperature and distance. I will try to define and illustrate this.

Elsewhere I have spelled out the view of language derived from the work of various grammarians and philosophers which seems language as moving on two levels—deep and superficial. The deep and more primitive roots (Wittgenstein, Langer) are essentially musical and function originally—in both the historic and developmental sense—for the communication of states of mind by the mechanism of projective identification (Bion). Upon this foundation there has gradually been built (and the child rapidly constructs) the lexical level for the conveying of information about the outside world. Finally, the poetic function finds the metaphoric means of describing the inner world through the forms of the external world. It is through the modulation of the interplay of these three levels that the means can be found for controlling the atmosphere of communication, the dimensions of which I wish to describe as temperature and distance.

If one imagines that the speaking voice could be modulated through its entire range musically, this would provide a spectrum stretching from monotone to full operatic splendour. In practice, of course, we neither can nor wish to do this but operate within a segment of this spectrum. Its elements would be the ordinary ones of music: tone, rhythm, key, volume and timbre. By modulating these musical elements, we can control the emotionality of the voice and thus what I mean by the temperature of our communication. This, in turn, has an impact on the emotional atmosphere of the consulting-room and the reverberation between patient and analyst, variously heightening or damping this atmosphere.

But the distance between the analyst and patient can also be modified from moment to moment. An awareness of splitting processes in the patient makes this possible, especially if we take note of the language differences between various parts of his personality when they present themselves directly at times of acting-in-the-transference. We can by this means utilize rather different languages as a directional advice, each different from the other in vocabulary, imagery drawn from the patient's speech and dreams, levels of education, degrees of vulgarity or refinement, etc. In addition to this directional device for addressing different parts of the patient's personality at different times, we can also modify the distance by not addressing the part concerned in our formulation at all, but rather, talking about that part to another, or by ruminating aloud in the presence of the patient, leaving it to his choice to listen or ignore.

Having now briefly described these two dimensions of technique in communication which are felt to lend themselves to ingenuity of modulation, it should be possible to make some more general statement about the principles that seem to guide the modulation itself, and then to illustrate this with some clinical material. Since the purpose of this modulating ingenuity is to free the analyst to share his thoughts with the patient without distorting the analytic process which has in its origins in the patient (that is, neither to lead nor to provoke, stimulate, confuse etc), and since the speed with which things happen in the consulting-room is too great for preconceived experimentation without serious loss of spontaneity and rapport, what I am going to describe is hindsight. It is an evaluation of the virtuosity—whether for good or ill—which I realize I have been evolving over the years and can now recognize as an established aspect of my technique. Of course there are the survivors of countless pieces of ingenuity, many of which have failed and needed to be guarded against in subsequent work. Naturally, I do not put these forward for others to adopt, but rather as a guide to help others to examine their own development of linguistic ingenuity. I think I can claim that the whole area is fairly free of methodological or theoretical preconception; but of course—being based to such a degree on hindsight – the attempts at generalization are open to wide error. But from my own point of view my interest in presenting such a paper for discussion is to elicit my colleagues' help in evaluating the crucial question: *do such ingenious devices, indeed, stay within the framework of basic technical method? In other words, where does ingenuity end and acting-in-the-transference begin?* I am, of course, claiming that I want my freedom in order to enrich the process and not for its own sake —to increase my pleasure in the work, etc. But we know well from

Freud the serious limitations and distortions that the unconscious transference can introduce, and that this manifests itself in the analyst, as does the transference in the patient, through difficulty in interposing thought between impulse and action. Freud's advice of the "blank-screen" demeanour and other technical restrictions had as one aim the minimizing of the danger of "wild analysis". This was a bit of do-as-I-say-and-not-as-I-do advice to the young; but strictures are in themselves unsuccessful, as is morality in other areas of life. The matter is too complicated to be settled by simple means. Not only (say) can acting be hidden in "blank-screen" demeanour, but the patient can easily take it as characterological rather than as formal or technical.

If, then, the methodological problem exists and cannot be side-stepped by rules of conduct, if we wish to free the analyst for the sake of enriching the communication qua communication, if we wish to accomplish this while still avoiding the pitfall of opening a Pandora's Box of acting-in-the-countertransference, then we must examine and formulate and evaluate what we actually find ourselves doing—to see if guiding principles can be formulated in lieu of constricting rules of conduct.

On close examination of my own technique, I think I can discern the operation of the following principles for the modulation of temperature and distance:

1. In the realm of the emotional music of the voice, it is my impression that I tend towards the centre, you might say. That is, if we envisage this emotional spectrum and the segment of it in which people actually operate, my contribution at any moment seems to function to bring the atmosphere back to the mean – generally damping ardour, and infusing vitality into languor. I notice that I tend to talk a bit more loudly than the whisperer and more softly than the shouter, less minor-key than the depressed and less major-key than the manic, more slowly than the galloper and faster than the tarrier, with less vibrato that the passionate, etc. Perhaps everyone does this naturally, automatically. But in fact I think not, for I know from myself and supervisees how easy it is to be swept on or retarded by the

atmosphere created by patients who are powerful projectors: how tempting it is to simulate empathy by mimicry. I believe that major difficulties in the analysis can result from the patient experiencing this as evidence of his success in omnipotently controlling the analyst.

2. With regard to the dimensions of distance, I have described two aspects—variations in the object of the communication, and variations of the direction. Perhaps I could categorize these more fully before trying to adduce general principles:

    a. The object may be either the adult part of the patient's personality or one or more infantile structures or a more generalized class of object of which some part of the patient is a member (men, children, babies etc.), and these may be referred to in the past, present or future.

    b. The direction of the communication may be described as direct to a particular part, indirect (to some part about another part), or directionless (simply put out into the room as an uncertain rumination that might possibly interest the patient or some part of him, though this seems unlikely at the moment.

I notice that I tend to modify these aspects of direction and object to regulate distance according to whether what I have to say seems likely to increase or diminish the pain in the patient's awareness at the moment. I am, of course, assuming that the pain is there and that the patient may or may not be suffering from it at the moment (Bion). In general, interpretations referable to persecutory anxiety are likely to diminish the pain, and those referable to depressive anxiety to increase the suffering at the moment. Therefore, I seem to be more likely to address an interpretation of persecutory anxiety directly to the part in pain, and more likely to talk to the adult part about a part that is suffering from depressive anxiety. Likewise, I notice that when problems of co-operation and responsibility are at issue, I seem to talk to the adult part about himself. The question of direction seems to be handled mainly linguistically, through differential vocabulary, partly derived from the patient's account of the parental language of his particular childhood, or cultural in origin where this information is lacking (mummy and daddy, pooh-pooh and wee-wee talk). I am willing to use the patient's own degree of vulgarity (fuck, shit, etc.) when addressing that part; to talk in simple language to the child in him; and at his maximum level of linguistic sophistication to the adult (or perhaps above, where his educational level is lower than his cultural aspirations).

I think I can go no further in exploring my own technique until presentation of some clinical material makes this possible. The best thing to do would be to present an example of successful modulation and also of an unsuccessful one. But as space is limited and what I consider "successful" will certainly be open to contrary construction, I will restrict myself to a single session. It is not verbatim, of course, but was constructed in the evening from an outline made in ten minutes immediately after the session. I will try to identify the modulatory linguistic shifts and to categorize them.

Clinical material

Mr G is a man of thirty, a sociologist doing research, and he comes to analysis partly for professional reasons. I see him four times per week, and he is approaching the end of his second year of treatment, hovering between breaking off the analysis as a fraud and becoming deeply devoted to it as the means of releasing him from being a "sod", a "selfish bastard". He had spent most of the previous session complaining about his mother. She is never pleased with him because she cannot boast of his achievements with confidence, as other mothers seem always to top her boasts of his status, income, or achievements. I had interpreted mainly that he seemed to accuse me of being such an analytic mother, using a carrot-and-stick technique. He had responded by complaining that no-one he knows who has had an analysis seems to him particularly admirable—although, of course, he has never met anyone treated by me.

But I seem to him to be always implying that my other patients are so much better, etc.

At the end of the session, after I had reminded him of an earlier Isaac-formulation—of how he wished to be the favourite by placing his life in my hands trustingly, even though he thought that I and psychoanalysis might be madly destructive—he left scowling and did not take his briefcase. It was only after he had left the house that I realized this, and knowing that he was in need of it, I took it out to him as he was turning his car. He had come twenty minutes late to the session through over-sleeping, and I had gone three minutes overtime and might have gone further, had he not looked at his watch.

The following session he came on time, entering with an aggressive look, and he launched immediately into a diatribe for about ten minutes. The substance of it was that I was always trying to make him feel inferior and guilty by my behaviour, so that it would seem that he was unfriendly while I was above reproach in my psychoanalytic decorum, so carefully thought out and meticulously applied. But it was clear yesterday, when I had handed him his case, that I was annoyed, because I did not say "welcome" to his "thank you" nor smiled to his smile. At first he had felt grateful and guilty for inconveniencing me, until he had recognized the truth of my annoyance.

ANALYST: That is, until you had courageously fought off these bad feelings that I was so ruthlessly projecting into you. (*ironic, with a slight laugh*) (*to the little boy, lightly*)

PATIENT: (*laughing against his will*) Yes, it's true. I'm not going to be bullied by you. That is exactly what happened.

ANALYST: It can only be an account of your experience and seems to have been retrospectively modified. Even so, you would not challenge the possibility of error in observation and judgement. For instance, the child in you may not have noticed that I had nodded in reply to your thanks; perhaps there was a smile in my eyes if not on my lips, just as you had not noticed when I held the briefcase up but continued to turn your car. (*serious, to the adult*)

PATIENT: I did notice you holding it up and was pleased. I thought it was a normal, friendly greeting, like "Hi, Joe", but I didn't realize it was my case. And that's why I was so shocked by your unfriendly behaviour when I opened the window and said, "Thank you".

ANALYST: Perhaps what was shocked and disappointed was the desire in the little boy for me to set aside my analytic technique as a sign of favouritism – to be the good mummy and daddy who never cause him the pain of jealousy of other good children. (*slightly teasing to the adult about the child, as shift towards baby-talk*)

PATIENT: Anyone would feel offended by such behaviour [trying to whip up anger again, but not very successfully.] The whole world says "Hello" and "goodbye" except you. Why can't you say "welcome" instead of just nodding? You are the unfriendly and out-of-step one (*warming to his task*). You hide it behind a façade of technical behaviour but in fact you treat your patients with contempt and try to make them feel inferior as a way of driving them to accept your theories and values. (*with triumphant finality*)

ANALYST: These values suggest that if you oversleep, if you leave your case behind, if you accept the benefits of analysis, you might feel some valuable guilt or unworthiness to spur your development. But if you do not distinguish between the valuable pains aroused by the goodness of your objects from the pains of persecution by your enemies, then it follows that anyone who causes you pain is an enemy. (*to the infantile structures generally, serious and a bit severe*)

PATIENT: (*smiling but sarcastic*) Then you'll like the dream I had last night and interpret it as confirmation, but I see it as a vindication of my courageous and pugnacious attitude to life. You remember I told you that my old boss was coming to lecture, and I had invited him to stay with us and was arranging a dinner-party for him. Well, David phoned to say he didn't need to trouble us to put him up as he had friends at Stanton St John.

ANALYST: (*dubious*) But that sounds fairly uncivilized. (*a bit teasing, to the adult*)

PATIENT: Yes, I realized it as I said it. That isn't really how it happened: I didn't contact him directly. He may not have known of our invitation until he'd already accepted the other. He's not a rude or ungrateful person, though he can be thoughtless and egocentric. I did feel hurt, but perhaps without good reason. My touchiness. Anyhow, in the dream I had gone into a bar, and someone just punched me on the nose. Well, I think he did—something hurt me, I think on the nose. So I put on boxing gloves and so did he, and we fought, and every punch I threw hit him on the face, and every one he threw missed me. But he didn't seem to get damaged somehow, and when David passed I commented on this to him. But then I noticed that instead of getting damaged, the other bloke seemed to get smaller and smaller, until it was clear that by continuing to fight I was just being a bully. So I suggested we stop, and anyhow I was no longer angry.

ANALYST: If every time mummy offers you her nipple you think she is flaunting the big penis she got from daddy during the last holiday, you are likely to feel justified in biting that nipple-penis. Only if mummy can bear this aggression without really striking back to things gradually assume their correct proportions. Then you can see it is a friendly little nipple, like the smile in her eyes. (*gently and softly, to the baby*)

(*Silence for three minutes*)

PATIENT: Well, there's nothing more to say. (*depressed*)

ANALYST: Ever? (*laughing*) (*lightly, to the baby*)

PATIENT: (*laughing*) You win again, I suppose.

ANALYST: But isn't that just the issue? Are we in a fight where someone wins and someone loses, or can we shift to another vertex where either we both win or we both lose, because our individual developments are at issue, not social triumph and superiority? (*serious, to the adult*)

(*Silence for three minutes*)

PATIENT: (*petulantly*) But my mother is like that, and she must have been that way all my life, since I was born, so it isn't surprising if I'm unfriendly and suspicious and view the world as a place of competition and ruthless fighting. So I'm not to blame. (*ends weakly, trailing off*)

ANALYST: But this material also suggests another possibility: that a baby who is still incontinent, as you were about oversleeping and leaving your case, may be unable to accept the kindness from the breast because, when it is in pain about the loss of control, feels little and humiliated. It experiences the pain as being put into it by a breast that uses the nipple to remind the baby of the daddy's big and continent penis. Your mother today does not relate herself to the baby in you, as I can do in the analysis, so perhaps her behaviour with you does not give a picture of her motherliness but of some level of girlish vanity. If you can begin to recognize different levels in yourself, you may also begin to recognize them in others as well. (*persuasive, to adult and baby simultaneously*)

This clinical material should now permit me to refine a bit the ideas put forward in the earlier sections. The method of psychoanalysis that Freud designed and developed is one, I firmly believe, of great beauty and humanity. Furthermore, it seems to me to combine a scientific means of making observations about a psychological situation to which precise modes of thought may then be applied for the sake of combining the single periods of observation into a longitudinal study. This can be raised to a high level of abstraction so that varied experiences may be combined to allow for valid generalization. But even more than this, it is a method that gives scope to both analyst and patient for creative artistic activity. One of the areas for this is that of technique—generally speaking, in the sensitive and tactful application of the basic principles. It can also allow—I am claiming—for an adventuresome exploration of the limits to which ingenuity can extend and render flexible and potent these basic principles, thus allowing patient and analyst to create between them a highly unique interaction that goes beyond mere practice and borders on art.

In the heat of the moment in the consulting-room or playroom, we have little time to make systematic observations of our technical functioning. But as experience grows and facility gives way to virtuosity as a manifestation of growth in our own personalities, a retrospective observation of the technical area becomes possible in repose. Naturally, it is wide open to falsification: error possibly increasing directly with the square of the distance in time from the session, but this is surely open to serial refinement of observation and thought. The questions in my mind upon which I would value discussion centre on two issues: (1) is the matter of this paper indeed worthy of being considered technical, or are these merely matters of style? And (2) what sort of criteria could be used for deciding whether we have crossed the border from the area of ingenuity within basic principles into the boundless infinite of acting-in-the-countertransference?

Finally, of course, there is the question of whether such a paper is of interest to one's colleagues or is essentially private. This is important, for it will also determine what we try to teach our students. If it is essentially private and essentially stylistic, I submit that it should not be taught, for it cannot be learned but only identified with. This carries the danger of narcissistic identifications in a supervisory situation where there is no means of either detecting or correcting the tendency, as one may hope to do with candidates in analysis. But that this is an area of private interest and concern, I am certain; for though we do gradually become skilful in doing what we know, our activity is of such a complex nature that we can only claim to know a little about what we do.

CHAPTER FOUR

A psychoanalytical model of the child-in-the-family-in-the-community

Introduction by Martina Campart

The work from which this extract is taken was commissioned from Donald Meltzer and Martha Harris in 1976 by the Organization for Economic and Cultural Development as part of a project to develop policies and programmes that would support families in their educational task.

The monograph presents a model of the learning processes as they take place in the child within the family within the community. The child's emotional, cognitive and social growth, as well as ethics and view of life, has its foundations in learning. We do not learn all in the same way and not all learning has the same value. *Learning from experience* is based on the ability to put up with uncertainty and mental pain, and promotes real growth. Other modes of learning, based on the denial of mental pain, are more imitative and superficial, and hinder or lead to a "fake" kind of development. These are classified as: learning by projective identification; by adhesive identification; by scavenging; delusional learning; and learning through submission to a persecutor.

Although the "favourite" mode of learning is related to individual temperament or endowment, the implementation of this potential through "learning habits" is related to the ways in which the family accomplishes its emotional and educational functions, in a process that is brought to completion at the end of adolescence. The group of functions that includes generating love, promoting hope, containing pain, and thinking, fosters learning from experience. The group that includes promulgating hate, sowing despair, emanating persecutory anxiety, and creating confusion, is likely to favour more destructive forms of learning and development. Meanwhile the family is also a learning system, sensitive to the surrounding social community. Therefore an analysis of which types of environment are supportive, and which disruptive, completes the Model's field of investigation.

The Model has been translated into several European languages, and during the 1980's and 90's was widely disseminated amongst therapists, teachers and teacher-trainers, social workers and similar professionals. Owing to its integration of a psychoanalytical theory of learning with an ecological conception of how the various systems involved in the educational process are interconnected, it is still of great present-day relevance, both to practitioners working in conditions of great complexity and to policy-makers.

The epistemological dimension of the model[1]
(1976)

This dimension of metapsychology is inherent in the later work of Wilfred Bion and the amplified model of the mind which he has superimposed on Freud's model as implicitly modified by Melanie Klein. It enables us to distinguish various categories of learning, to define the mental state underlying them,

---

[1] Extract from Meltzer & Harris, "A Psychoanalytic Model of the Child-in-the-Family-in-the-Community", written in 1976 for the Organization of Economic and Cultural Development of the United Nations, and first published in English in A. Hahn (ed.) *Sincerity: Collected Papers of Donald Meltzer* (1994), pp. 392-94.

and to trace their consequences for personality development. They may be named learning from experience, from projective identification, from adhesive identification, from scavenging, from delusion. All contrast with *learning about*.

Learning from experience, as described by Bion (1965), involves participation in an emotional experience in such a way that a modification of the personality takes place. The person "becomes" something that he was not before, say a "walker" in the case of a small child, or a "doctor" in the case of an adult. Internal qualification of this sort may be contrasted with the varieties of external qualification bestowed by social structures.

In contrast, *learning by projective identification* involves an omnipotent phantasy of entry into, and taking over, the mental qualities and capabilities of another person. Because the conception of the other person is limited and since the projection imbues him with qualities of the subject, the result is something of a caricature. Where the projective identification is with an internal object, qualities of omniscience and judgmental attitudes predominate.

On the other hand, in *learning by adhesive identification*, which involves a deeply unconscious phantasy of sticking on to the surface of the object, the resulting identification picks out only the social appearance and thus takes on the attributes of a somewhat mindless imitation of appearance and behaviour. It is characterised by instability, tending to collapse easily under stress and to be fickle, easily shifting to new objects of immediate interest or attachment.

Learning by scavenging typifies the envious part of the personality which cannot ask for help nor accept it with gratitude. It tends to view all skill and knowledge as essentially secret and magical in its control of nature and people. It watches and listens for items "thrown away", as it were, where no "please" or "thank you" need enter in, and therefore tends to feel triumphant over the stupidity of others for giving away the formula.

Delusional learning is of an entirely different order, believing that whatever is revealed in nature or by man is essentially worthless and that only the hidden and therefore occult is of value.

It sees evidence in the nuances while neglecting the apparent and constructs a world that is essentially anti-nature.

All five of these forms of learning are essentially autonomous in their inception and express either the thirst for knowledge and understanding, or its converse, intrusive curiosity. By contrast, learning about the world has its source in the motives of the teacher. Its methods are essentially those of animal training, stick-and-carrot, dependant for their success on co-opting greed, timidity, docility or competitiveness of the subject. Its achievements effect no deep modification of the person but rather decorate his social persona for purposes of adaptation to the demands of the environment, and have little connection with ultimate goals or ethical principles.

Of these six forms of learning only the first, learning from experience, requires a shift in values in keeping with the move from the paranoid-schizoid to the depressive position. It is heavily dependent on the assistance and guidance of benevolent objects (either internal or external) with whom it can share the burden of the anxiety, (confusional or persecutory), attending the impact of a new idea. The advent of the depressive feeling resulting from the changed view of self and world inherent in such learning is accompanied by feelings of gratitude and privileged indebtedness to the mentor.

The structural dimension of the model[i]

Temperament

The innate disposition of the individual is hardly definable by means of the psycho-analytical method of research but tends to be thought of as comprised of two categories: one being a set of innate preconceptions which await experiences that approximate to them so that they may grow into conceptions and concepts

---

i Extract from Meltzer & Harris, "A Psychoanalytic Model of the Child-in-the-Family-in-the-Community", in Hahn (ed.) 1994, pp. 395-401.

(Bion, Money-Kyrle); the second, a set of innate balanced inclinations, which may be strongly bound to the general physiology and may thus vary in life according to shifts in the psychological state. They may be described, for instance, by various dualities such as active-passive, masculine-feminine, violent-placid, reflective-outgoing, slow-fast. They may be thought to declare themselves in some degree at birth and immediately thereafter, or even to some extent in pre-natal activity, but these estimates are rendered uncertain by the unanswered, perhaps unanswerable question: "when does life-experience begin?" Given its imponderable aspect, the cautious observer will be reluctant to assign great significance to it on the basis of history of infantile development. The danger is that it may be used as a waste-basket for explaining-away, and for thus obscuring the extent of our ignorance. It corresponds to Freud's concept of the Id insofar as he meant "instinct" but not insofar as he meant "mental representation of bodily states". The concept of "self" is taken to be the functional, if not the most poetic, theoretical unit of structure in the mind and is seen to comprise both ego and id aspects in respect of both functions and representations of bodily states, the latter being subsumed under the general perceptual functions of the self.

So the temperament may be viewed as innate equipment, standing in relation to the self as the natural resources of a country stand in relation to the human community. Or perhaps a more accurate analogy would be: as the total physical environment, given by nature and history, stand in relation to the new generation. This gathers together the physiological-anatomical equipment and the mental inheritance.

Internal object organization

This level of structure moves towards stability with time and may be taken as the basis of mood. The internal objects fluctuate in various ways which lend themselves to fairly minute and precise study through the dreams of adults and the play of children. The parameters of variation are along lines of integration (partial or whole objects), degree of relatedness (separated or combined objects), beauty, goodness, truthfulness, dependability, strength, attentiveness, intelligence, emotional richness, and on a spectrum from harsh to gentle with respect to the ethical aegis they evoke in the mind (conscience). They may be damaged from cruel attacks from infantile parts of the personality, but can repair one another, even restore one another to life, given the proper emotional climate (depressive anxiety). Sexuality, reproduction, and the nurturing of the mother's internal and external babies are their overwhelming preoccupation.

They may be identified with by parts of the self in various ways; one form, introjective identification, giving rise to the adult part of the personality. But they may also be invaded, taken over, corrupted by the destructive part of the personality. In its most malignant form this produces the sadistic superego (Freud) or the "super"-ego (Bion).

The view taken here is that "learning from experience" (Bion) occurs where a new idea is assimilated by the internal combined object which then helps the self to master it and the emotional upheaval which attends its advent (Meltzer).

The adult organization

While infantile structures are in direct contact with the physiological state and the needs arising there, the adult structure of the personality is only indirectly related, in much the same way as parents were concerned with the physiological state of the infant and child.

The direct relation of the adult structure is to the internal objects with whom it is identified in an aspirational sense, as to teachers or mentors. This relation may be externalised in the form of an adult transference, as in religious belief, or to inspiring figures in the outside world, current or historic.

Its degree of integration of masculine and feminine attributes of mind is directly dependent on the state of integration of the internal objects; identification with the combined object being a precondition for creative mental functioning. The parental ethic of work and responsibility for the world and its children, human, animal or vegetable, is its central preoccupation and the source of its joy. Its capacity for loving companionship in sexuality generates the family, while its capacity for friendly co-operation makes the work-group (Bion) possible. It begins to form early in childhood.

The infantile organization

In its simplified form the infantile organization may be thought of as consisting of the boy-girl-, baby-, destructive- and schizophrenic parts of the personality. But these basic parts are subject to defensive splitting processes and may be multiplied or confused. Furthermore the distribution of capabilities may be unequal amongst the parts with respect to such qualities as intelligence, strength, and the other qualities mentioned under temperament.

But it is the distribution of strength (meaning essentially, tolerance to mental pain) and intelligence (particularly imaginativeness and speed, with special reference to verbal facility) which determines their dominance in the organization at infantile levels.

The destructive part is always in competition with the good objects for the leadership and naturally makes capital of every separation situation to establish its hegemony, exploiting all the techniques of propaganda, seduction and threat to dominate the other infantile parts. It is the liar, the bully, the cynic, the corrupter. It exploits the jealousy, intolerance to mental pain and the ignorance of the other parts to impose its authority, claiming omniscience (the know-it-all) and omnipotence (the capacity to achieve its ends by the power of its wish, without regard to the techniques of implementation).

It is deeply opposed to examining the meaning of things and is therefore inclined to insist that only external objects exist (denial of psychic reality) and that things are only what they seem. People may therefore be taken as the summation of their observable behaviour. It therefore promotes transference relations (that is, the externalisation of relations to the internal parents) to inadequate objects which it can discredit, collecting dossiers and insisting that the future may be foretold as a direct extrapolation of the past. Its tendency is to form the delinquent gang from its infantile cohort, but given sufficient success it becomes grandiose and establishes the Basic Assumption Group (Bion).

The family organization

Considering that each member of a family group, limited and extended, may be thought of in terms of the personality core just described, it is clear that a number of different principles of organization may operate to produce very different milieux for growth and education of its members. From the point of view of this model it is necessary to put to one side the nominal structure of families in order to describe their real psycho-social arrangement, both with respect to roles (titular) and functions (actual). Taking each member as a human being, unfettered by the pre-conceptions on stereotype, it is possible in studying a family group to recognise the actual organization of functions and to notice its interaction with the preservation of titular roles.

We are differentiating only four levels of family organization: the parental family; the matriarch-patriarchy; the gang; and the reverse or negative family. Under conditions which will be discussed later the family may lose its sophistication and become more primitive or tribal, both internally and *vis-à-vis* the community, showing the characteristics of one of the three Basic Assumption Groups (BaDep, BaF-Fl, BaP) (Bion).[i]

Basic assumption organization

Following Bion, we are taking the view that the more primitive form of organization, characterised by sharing of an unconscious

---
[i] Bion's three basic assumption groups are Dependency, Fight-Flight and Pairing.

primal myth and implemented by communication through projective identification (action and non-lexical level of language), can be seen to be present although not always active or obvious. Its unanimity of mind and speed of action stand in marked contrast to the progressive importance of thought and judgement as more sophisticated organization forms, accompanied by increased reluctance to act before adequate communication and conference has taken place.

Community organization

This model limits itself to the consideration of four different orientations of the community and the individual-in-the-family towards one another; each being an outgrowth of selection and interaction. We may take it that selection is in all but the most extreme cases of political tyranny, the prime operative factor in both directions. By and large we would view the impetus as arising in the family towards the community, but this may be reversed where prejudice is strong.

Again following Bion's use of the terms (*Attention and Interpretation*, 1970) we will call these orientations: commensal, symbiotic, parasitic and paranoid; assuming that in each case—selection, evocation and provocation being what they are—the relationship of family to community will be found to be mutual.

CHAPTER FIVE

Money-Kyrle's concept of misconception

Introduction by Jon Morgan Stokkeland and Lars Thorgaard

How is it that a concept, such as Money-Kyrle's of "misconceptions", can be of such extreme importance for our understanding of the psychoanalytic attitude? Meltzer poses the question, and he also gives elements of the answers, in this important discussion of Money-Kyrle's paper on "Cognitive Development". He writes with tenderness and care about the influence that Money-Kyrle had both personally and professionally on himself, on his own work and on his psychoanalytic attitude.

Psychoanalytic theory, he writes, is influenced by "harsh and puritanical aspects that can enter in such a judgemental way into our work". Meltzer wants us to use the concept of misconception to "increase the awareness of the complexity and the ineffable aspects of our work" and to help us "to distance ourselves even further from the vice of explanation, contenting ourselves with description and partial comprehension". Money-Kyrle's paper suggests "that innocent, unintentional misunderstandings, based on primal misconceptions growing out of early developmental experience, can seriously distort the entire structure of 'cognitive development'" [our italics].

For Meltzer the "special charm of this concept is its non-judgemental quality". This quality, embedded in his key use of the words "innocent" and "unintentional", expresses the very essence of the psychoanalytic attitude. Meltzer imbibed this attitude from his personal experience of Roger Money-Kyrle and it is exemplified in the way he writes about him. We believe Meltzer would agree that the analyst's non-judgemental attitude is of paramount importance in psychoanalytic practice. An inner voice constantly recalls Meltzer's words in one of his seminars: "I only speak to the patient, when I feel the sunshine in my voice". When Meltzer writes of Money-Kyrle that "his method of work in the consulting-room, his technique of teaching in supervision as well as the atmosphere of his written works all bear witness to the sort of humility that recoiled from sitting in judgement on his fellow men", he paints a portrait that we would apply to Meltzer himself, and our debt to him is the equivalent of his, as he expressed it, to Money-Kyrle.

Money-Kyrle's concept of misconception[i]
(1981)

With his extraordinary capacity to go directly to the heart of the matter, Roger Money-Kyrle has described the three epochs of psychoanalytic development—his own and the science's—with these references to the concept of mental illness:

1896-1930: "Mental illness is the result of sexual inhibitions."

---

[i] Extracts from the beginning and end of Meltzer, "Does Money-Kyrle's concept of misconception have any descriptive power?", published in the *Scientific Bulletin of the British Psychoanalytical Society* (1981) and reprinted in A. Hahn (ed.) *Sincerity: Collected Papers of Donald Meltzer* (1994), pp. 496-513.

1930-1960: "Mental illness is the result of unconscious moral conflict."

1960 to the present: "The patient, whether clinically ill or not, suffers from unconscious misconceptions and delusions."

He goes on with his characteristic modesty to explain that he is hoping to outline a theory of "cognitive development" that merely aspires to fashion "two hooks to hang a lot of existing theories on". In this paper I wish to examine the possibility that the theory of "misconception" may be a new idea with considerable descriptive power that other psychoanalytic theories do not possess. He explains:

> The two hooks relate to the two mental tasks any new-born animal has to perform if it is to survive: the acquisition of a few, I believe innately pre-determined, concepts (or class notions), and, what is not innately pre-determined, the location of their members in a space-time system.[i]

In the pages that follow in that brilliant paper, Money-Kyrle examines "concept building" and "system building" from a point of view based on Bion's work on thinking, but resting on a foundation of Melanie Klein's schizoid mechanisms and Freud's (1911) "Formulations on the Two Principles of Mental Functioning":

> What actually seems to happen is that, while part of the developing personality does learn to understand the facts of life, suffers the pains of an Oedipus complex, discards it from guilt, becomes reconciled to the parental relation, internalizes it and achieves maturity, other parts remain ignorant and retarded. (Money-Kyrle 1978, p. 421)

The ways in which a part of the personality (or the whole) may become "cognitively retarded" are investigated both in terms of the necessity for individual concepts to proceed from concrete to ideographic to conscious verbal representations and for systems of concepts of both an external and an internal world to evolve:

---

[i] R. Money-Kyrle, "Cognitive Development", read to the British Psycho-Analytical Society in 1967, published in the *International Journal of Psycho-Analysis* vol. 49, 1968), reprinted with a postscript in Meltzer (ed.)*Collected Papers of Roger Money-Kyrle* (1978), p. 417.

> From the beginning, the capacity to retain a memory of the external world system seems to depend on a capacity to internalize the base, at first in a very concrete way. (p. 425)

This base, Money-Kyrle suggests, "appears not to be normally the body-ego, but something to which the body-ego orients itself as its 'home'." This "home" must be, in the beginning, the nipple as "the O of the co-ordinate geometry of the mind".

But this "home", the "O" of the co-ordinate geometry of the mind, can be lost in several ways:

> I am not concerned at the moment with the ways in which the good base can turn "bad" by the infant projecting his own aggression into it so that it is misrecognized as bad. Apart from this the orientation to the good base can be lost in at least three ways: the baby can get into it by total projective identification, either out of envy or as an escape from a persecuting outer world; he can get orientated to the wrong base, in the sense that it is not the one he really needs; or he can become confused in his orientation because his base is confused with a part of his own body. (p. 425)

Money-Kyrle acknowledges that the "wrong base" and the "confused base" are not easily distinguished and furthermore, that the processes that lead to them are obscure. This paper will now try to explore this obscure area and, as stated, to examine whether this concept is merely "a hook to hang existing theories on" or a new theory with a new descriptive power. I am going to suggest that it is a new theory that opens the way to the exploration of processes of mother-baby (and thus of analyst-analysand) interaction that lie beyond the descriptive power of our existing theories, including Bion's Grid and his putative Negative Grid. The jumping-off place for this examination lies in Money-Kyrle's own postscript to the paper on "Cognitive Development" written in 1967, where he examines the implications of Bion's concept of maternal reverie. In the course of examining the beautiful dream of the motherly woman who gave the patient a bag to put in the box so that it would not spill out the prickly pine-needles, Money-Kyrle writes:

And if I am right, this is what happens in normal development: the infant finds a breast to cry into, and in turn gets back from it his distress in a detoxicated form which is capable of being stored and recalled, if necessary, as an element in thought. (p. 432)

He suspected there had been a maternal failure of reverie in the case of this patient, due to her mother's depression.

Existing theories seem to go some considerable distance in enabling us to describe the "normal" course of development and the interaction of pathological aspects of the developing child *vis-à-vis* its intimate surroundings, both in its normal (or better, "optimal") and "inadequate" aspects. But this is only taking into consideration the intentional aspects of the behaviour of figures in the environment. It is like describing a painting only in its iconographic aspects, without reference to the mysterious compositional qualities wherein its unique impact on the viewer resides. Similarly, our powers of describing the analytic situation tend to be limited to descriptions of the content—emotional and fantasy—of the transference and countertransference. May this be the mere "iconography" of the analytic situation—throwing very little light on the development of the treatment situation and its overall impact on the lives of analyst and analysand? In a paper read to the European Psychoanalytical Association in 1976,[i] I explored some of the more "compositional" aspects of the analytic situation in an attempt to extend the scope of our observation of our functioning in the consulting-room thinking that a wider range of self-observation by the analyst could also increase his technical mastery of his behaviour in keeping with the individual patient's needs. In that paper, two particular "dimensions" of interaction, interpersonal "temperature" and "distance" were examined. In the material I am about to present in order to examine the utility of the concept "misconception", the dimension of "relative speed" of mental functioning and behaviour between mother and baby (analyst and analysand) will be considered.[ii]

---

[i] "Temperature and distance as technical dimensions of interpretation"; see this volume, Chapter 3.
[ii] For reasons of space the clinical material that follows has had to be omitted.

[*Clinical material omitted*]

The task now remains to investigate the implications of Money-Kyrle's concept of misconception in order to discover why it seems to me to break new ground, or at least to widen the emotional-ethical scope of our investigations of human mentality, development, and relationships. A brief historical survey would appear to be in order at this point—a personal one, to be sure, and therefore not one with which all analysts would agree.

It appears to me that, despite his expressed wish to avoid putting forward a theory of the mind that embraced a particular *weltanschauung*, Freud was unable to avoid it. The overall picture of the human condition inherent in his theories, both the early topographic and the later structural, is of a mechanical apparatus seeking equilibrium, battered by stimuli from within and without—the "three masters" described most explicitly in *The Ego and the Id* (1923). Both "death theory" and "Nirvana principle" make it clear that "pleasure" is negative in its significance—the release from the "unpleasure" of "accretions of stimuli". While the manifestations of the problem of adaptation may seem to be full of meaning, the problem itself is seen as essentially mechanical, and therefore meaningless.

Melanie Klein's determination to follow the lead of the children whose phantasies she observed—namely, to treat the internal world as a fact as concrete in its meaning for the mind as were the facts of the physical world for the body—brought her ideas into the philosophical areas of Platonism, where meaning was to be seen as a creation of the mind. This evocation of an internal world as a theatre for the generating of meaning increased the complexity of the phenomena that could be discerned in the consulting-room, by multiplying the number of "worlds" that could be brought into view by the transference. The transformation of the concept of narcissism from a directional aspect of the libido into a structural and organizational one referable to infantile structures, brought in its wake a renewed optimism as regards both theory and prophylaxis. Childhood development might be seen as biologically programmed, as Freud saw it, but the programming took on a new hopefulness so long as it took place within a benign environment. The family became a kind of hot-house in which baby plants might grow and blossom, be gradually "hardened off", and enter the raw atmosphere of the culture with great survival capacity, once the good internal objects were secured within the depressive position.

But this early optimism did not long survive the bold excursions into the psychoanalytic treatment of the more severe disorders. The outcome was the theory of envy and a revival of the concept of negative therapeutic reaction. The canker had entered the rose, the snake into the garden, and with this it was revealed that a puritanical conception had indeed lurked behind this benign early vision: that the struggle between good and evil in the soul of man was, after all, the final arbiter. Bion's work did nothing to dispel this harsh view by its dissection of thinking—evoking the conflict between truth and lies as the phenomenology of the conflict between love and hate, life and death, truth and falsehood, the food or poison of the mind. The "foul fiend" still lurked in the underbrush.

I would suggest that such a view has lost what the Renaissance rediscovered: namely, the Hellenic view of tragedy, of the human condition overwhelmed by forces of which it is not only ignorant, but essentially innocent. This is not to be confused with the ample tragic aspect of Freud's view which, however, seems rather to embrace the Romantic Agony of the individual versus the group —essentially external. I would wish to suggest that Money-Kyrle's concept of misconception opens the way for investigation of factors of innocent misunderstanding between people based upon discontinuity in their conceptual frame of reference—the "O" of their mental analytic geometry.

I realize, of course, that a paper of this sort cannot be convincing in its clinical demonstration for the very reason that what it is attempting to evoke is essentially negative: the absence of intentionality as a factor in interpersonal conflict and developmental distortion. But while it cannot convince, it can suggest. It can suggest that innocent, unintentional misunderstandings based on primal misconceptions growing out of early developmental experience can seriously distort the entire structure of cognitive development. While the importance of this for clinical therapeutic work may not be very great—that would remain to be seen—its importance for the psychoanalytic attitude may be extensive. I would suggest that by merely allowing this concept to enter into our framework of thought, we soften the harsh and puritanical aspects of theory that can enter in such a judgemental way into our work. Perhaps by increasing our awareness of the complexity and the ineffable aspects of our work, it can help us to distance ourselves even further from the vice of explanation, contenting ourselves with description and partial comprehension.

The question will arise: what is the importance of this increment [the concept of misconception] to our descriptive tools?[i] The material presented in this paper suggests to me that it opens up areas of developmental processes hitherto inaccessible to description. Psychoanalytic theories of development have always emphasized the impact of the environment upon the constitutional tendencies of the individual child. To this viewpoint of Freud's there was added by Melanie Klein the viewpoint that took account of the schizoid mechanisms of splitting and projective identification. This introduced the problem of confusion: confusions of value, of geography, of identity, and of zones and modes of interaction between self and object. Bion has added the dimension of disturbances in thought processes, and the constant conflict between the desire to discover the truth and the tendency to employ the capacity for fabricating lies in order to evade the pain connected with the truth. I wish to suggest that Money-Kyrle's concept of misconception introduces a dimension in developmental factors—and thus a viewpoint about development—that goes outside the realm of conflict about meaning. It makes an approach to the aspects of emotional sympathy and alienation between individuals that is surely at its root emotional, but for which we have virtually no accepted descriptive language. Vague words like "congenial", "*simpatico*", "*gemütlich*", "*agréable*", do not go very far in exploring the content or basis of empathic bonding in human relationships.

---

[i] The following paragraphs represent "a second ending to the [original] paper" (Hahn 1994, [ed.], p. 512).

Perhaps the special charm of this concept is its non-judgemental quality. My personal experience of Roger Money-Kyrle over the years is deeply connected with this special quality. His method of work in the consulting room, his technique of teaching in supervision as well as the atmosphere of his written works, all bear witness to the sort of humility that recoiled from sitting in judgement on his fellow men. While he had a deep sense of the role of evil in conflict with good with regard to internal processes, he was nonetheless convinced that the huge proportion of people wished to live in peace and amity with one another. And he was convinced that they would do so some day when the many minsunderstandings that divide them against one another—parents against children, husbands against wives, ethnic and political groups in conflict—were clarified. It was his firm belief that psychoanalysis, arm in arm with philosophy and the social sciences, art, and literature, would eventually succeed in this task. Nor was it simply an expression of a sanguine disposition. It arose from his experience of life, in peace and in war, and was continually strengthened by his experience in the analytic consulting-room.

CHAPTER SIX

The delusion of clarity of insight

Introduction by Tomas Plänkers

The Claustrum (in which this paper is reprinted) is a compendium of Meltzer's inspiring theoretical and clinical thinking. One of his late works, it demonstrates yet again his creative capacity to bring into flower the germinal Kleinian concepts.

Melanie Klein in her paper on schizoid mechanisms (1946) linked paranoid anxieties with the oral sadistic impulses in little children, which deprive the mother's body of its good contents and deposit the child's faeces inside her in order to control her internally. Insofar as mother now contains the bad parts of the baby, she is no longer experienced as a separate object: she is now the bad self. Based on these findings about projective identification and on Abraham's papers on the anal character (1923), Meltzer in his paper on the relationship of anal masturbation and projective identification (1966) mapped out a special Kleinian contribution to the concepts of narcissism and autoerotism. His central idea circled around projective identification with internal objects:

masturbatory activities stimulate phantasies of intruding into the object, destroying what is assumed to be the cause of psychic pain and controlling it.

Following W. R. Bion's findings on the geography of psychic processes, Meltzer outlined the internal world of the internal mother for the first time in *Explorations in Autism* (1975), later in *Dream-Life* (1984) and in *Studies in Extended Metapsychology* (1986). In *The Claustrum* (1992) he gives a fascinating account of the three compartments of the world inside the internal mother that can be entered by intrusive identification: the head-breast (as in the "delusion of clarity of insight"), the genital, and the anal compartments. Living unconsciously in any of these has severe psychopathological consequences. Meltzer's investigations in these narcissistic worlds profoundly enlarge our understanding of schizophrenia, borderline states, perversions, addictions and claustrophobic phenomena. As a result our comprehension of the specifics of transference and countertransference while dealing with these patients has to be changed and is described in detail. Furthermore the social psychological understanding of groups, organizations and politics benefits deeply from this unique approach to the internal world. The book concludes with an impressive analysis of equivocation in Shakespeare's *Macbeth* by Meg Harris Williams— demonstrating the far-reaching utility of the Claustrum concept beyond the clinical field.

The delusion of clarity of insight[i]
(1976)

To implement his sensory equipment, tool-making man became scientific-man and developed an astonishing range of instruments for evaluating quantities in the external world. He developed an adequate notational system for assisting his memory and communication about these objects.

---
[i] First published in 1976 in the *International Journal of Psycho-analysis*, and reprinted in Meltzer, *The Claustrum* (1992), pp. 73-85.

Emboldened by this signal success, in the last century particularly, he began to try—with understandable optimism—to apply these same techniques to the description and measurement of the things of which his inner world, psychic reality, is composed.

The consequent output of instruments and data has again been impressive, but many people feel uneasy about the value and precision of these products, for in some way they seem to fall so short in richness as well as meaningfulness, of the instruments for investigation and communication developed by poets, artists, musicians and theological figures. Some people feel that it is the conceptual background that is to blame and not the instruments. Others felt that we have come up against the limitations of language—trying, as Wittgenstein (1953) claims, to say things that can only be shown. Freud noted quite early (Breuer and Freud, 1893-5) a very striking split in his own use of language: that his theories rang of the laboratory and his data read like short stories. As he went on with his work he also noted over and over that, when faced with conceptual impasse, he found himself returning to the dream as his primary datum (Freud, 1918).

This seems to be a lesson of which it is easy to lose sight. We can forget that our patients, and ourselves, present a unique language in dreams, a language whose substance shapes the content, if not the aesthetic essence, of art. Dreams borrow the forms of the external world and suffuse them with the meaning of the internal world. We do, with practice, learn to read this dream-language in ourselves and our patients with some fluency, even at times with virtuosity. With its help we find a vocabulary and a music for interpretation that are at once highly personal and mysteriously universal. Our use of this dream-palette underlies the claim that psychoanalysis is truly an art-form, in itself, quite outside the question of whether any of us are good—let alone great—artificers in its employment. In this method we operate with intuitive insights supervised by scientific, conscious modes of observation and thought. It is a method which is rich enough in its potentialities to allow for the possibility of inspiration and great beauty to emerge.

In this artistic activity supervised by scientific functions the latter are deployed in several echelons. First perhaps we try to see that a formulation "covers" the material at hand. Then, in repose, we may estimate its harmony with previous material and interpretation. Subsequently we estimate its consequences for the emergence of new material and the evolution of a process. But our strength of conviction does not, I suggest, come from this wedding of insight and judgement. It comes rather from the aesthetic component of the experience—the "beauty" with which the material and the formulation cohabit, blossom, fruit as a thing apart from ourselves.

In this slow process the richness with which interpretive possibilities arise in an analyst's mind plays a paradoxical role. While this richness lengthens the time span over which conviction must ripen and beauty emerge, the durability of the conviction is proportionately enhanced. But we can notice times at which quite another process takes place in ourselves, one which we may even confuse with inspiration. Naturally it comes more readily to our notice in our patients, and I have come to think of it as the "delusion of clarity of insight". It, too, bears off-spring—but not ones of beauty. Its favourite child is called "sitting-in-judgement". Others such as smugness, superciliousness, aloofness and pride follow quickly on.

It is just this juxtaposition and the basis of shifting between these two types of functioning that I wish to explore and exemplify, for I suspect that identification processes and the shift from introjective to narcissistic modes are at its root. I say "narcissistic" identifications rather than "projective" identification (Klein, 1946) because I am not at all sure that the latter is the only means of its—the shift's —achievement. But as you will see, my material points only to a specific aspect of projective identification, one which is bound up closely with the epistemophilic instinct. Where the thirst for knowledge is still strongly dominated by motives related to envy and jealousy, it is impatient of learning either from experience, example or demonstration. It seeks rather the immediate emotional satisfaction of omniscience and this it accomplishes by intruding inside the sensory apparatus and mental equipment of its internal object. Here are three clinical vignettes to illustrate this:

Case A

A medical student had noticed recently a sharp deterioration in his capacity for clinical observation and thought during the course of an analytical break. He brought a dream that *he and his wife were walking along a country road admiring the scenery, and then they were driving in a car along a causeway between two bodies of water. Suddenly the car stopped and he realized that he had gone too far and had broken off the rubber hose which connected his car to the petrol pump.*

The point of the dream seems to be that when he is in projective identification (driving the car) his appreciation of the complexity and beauty of the data (the landscape) is narrowed to one-track-mindedness and simple ideas of causality (the causeway) until he recognizes the need for the analysis (fuel pump) to help him get beyond his present limitations.

Case B

A young author in his fifth year of analysis was struggling with his genital Oedipus conflict, his dependence upon the analysis and upon his internal objects for the continuation of his creative powers. The prospect of termination of the analysis had come in sight and tended to throw him into a confusion of identity with his little daughter and the problem of having a second child. He dreamed that *he was with a colleague* (long recognized to be linked with the analyst) *inside a dome-like conservatory* (like the one he had been admiring near the Heath the previous day) *discussing his new book. When the colleague suggested that the two main sections of the book should be more creatively linked together in a geographical way, the patient was suddenly disturbed by a droning sound. When he looked up the sky was crowded with transparent objects, a mixture of Luftwaffe and fireflies. He felt he must rush home to protect his little girl from the bombs.*

The dream seemed strongly to imply that the moment the analyst suggests that his internal objects might be allowed to come together to create a new baby, the patient's delusion-of-clarity-of-insight (inside the conservatory-breast) recognizes that this would be dangerously destructive to the little-girl part of himself and that she must be protected from such an experience at all costs. It would only bombard her with Nazi-envy and preoccupation with daddy's exciting genitals (fireflies).

Case C

A young woman seemed unable to make any progress in analysis owing to shallowness of a latency-period type in which she was waiting-for-daddy-to-come-and-marry-her. This had firmly attached itself to the analyst-daddy in such a way that no interpretation was taken seriously for its content but only as a countertransference activity expressing either loving or sadistic erotism. After visiting her brother's family for the weekend she dreamed that *she was taking a little boy up in a lift and kissing him, but she was somewhat afraid that her breath might smell bad*. This dream was construed to mean that she had got inside the analyst-mummy at the weekend to steal her babies, but was worried that her love was contaminated by her anal sadism reflected in her addiction to smoking.

The following night she dreamed that she was inside a glass conservatory protecting a little boy from Cary Grant, who seemed to be a raving homosexual intent on whipping the boy with his extraordinarily long penis. As I interpreted to her at some length (*sic!*) that she had shifted from stealing the babies from the mummy to being one of these inside-babies masochistically submitted to the sadistic tongue-penis of the erotic daddy, the patient mainly giggled and smirked and asked why I was so serious, why was I so excited, that my interpretation seemed disappointingly unoriginal, that I was probably hurt by her lack of admiration for my mind, etc. Clearly I was unable to shift her from her state of projective identification inside the breast (conservatory) from which position the delusion-of-clarity-of-insight into the analyst's state of mind showed her unequivocally that he was hurt, excited, and sadistically whipping her with long interpretation-penises.

Clearly such examples are too anecdotal and unconvincing. They can only exemplify, leaving many doubts and unanswered questions. The broad landscape narrowing to the causeway may suggest an impoverished imagination in Case A. The simplification of modes of thought from complex linking to simple causality may be implied. The dome-shaped conservatory suggests the breast and the Luftwaffe-fireflies may indeed imply a high degree of omniscience in Case B. The fact that Case C is dependent on her spectacles to a degree that far outstrips her refractive error may be linked with going up in the lift, as a means of getting inside the mother's conservatory head-breast to look at the world through her eyes. But it is all only suggestive on its own. To find greater conviction as well as a richer conception of the role of such operations in a person's life-style we must look at a more longitudinal picture of an analysis.

Case D

This handsome woman in her 40's was well along in her career as a research chemist, successfully combined with marriage and children, when she came to analysis in some despair about her bad temper with the children, picking at her forehead and compulsive eating of chocolate. Her relationship with Mr D seemed to have progressively deteriorated since they had spent an extraordinarily happy and fruitful year in Canada, each working in their somewhat related fields. From the outset she was extremely sceptical about analysis and felt that, of the many people she knew in London who had been analysed, the only one who showed distinct improvement in Mrs D's eyes was paradoxically the least enthusiastic about the method.

From the outset the work was continually confronted by a minute questioning of the validity of the method by this highly intelligent and observant woman. It was not done in a hostile way but was presented as necessary to her giving a more faultless co-operation. This indeed she did, superficially, but her attitudes suggested and underlying negativism and she admitted feeling little hope of benefit. However, she felt she could not resign herself in good conscience to the peculiarities of her character, since they affected the children, not to mention her husband's happiness, until every reasonable effort had been made. In a sense the analyst had to maintain the working-level of hopefulness and bear the full burden of the hopelessness which constantly recurred. He and analysis were put to the test while the patient waited with rather exquisitely balanced wishes for the distant outcome. When it transpired that the presenting complaints were only small fragments of her character and symptom pathology, no improvement in other areas was granted status. Her irritability only grew worse until it finally metamorphosed by the third year into a diffuse indifference and lovelessness towards everyone. In her tally-book the analysis had only made her worse and indeed gave every promise of completely wrecking her life. Yet, paradoxically, she had no desire to leave, but rather showed every sign of settling in for the duration—of her or my life, whichever was the shorter. In the face of this daunting loss of interest—in work, children, sexuality, social life—it was necessary to hold fast to the rigging of the analysis and its internal evolution.

But in fact the development of the analytical material, the evolution of the transference and the patient's growing understanding of mental processes left nothing to be desired, except for pleasure and enthusiasm on her part. An early intense erotic transference had exhibited very clear voyeuristic elements. A strong desire to look at the analyst, minute monitoring of his noises, smells and appearance as well as those of the rest of the house, all accompanied by intense oceanic emotionality at times, seemed—as illustrated by her dreams—to point to the impact of early experiences in the parental bedroom. Secretiveness proliferated, along with a rather paranoid attitude about the possibility of being recognized going to or coming from the analyst's rooms. She kept the analysis an absolute secret from her mother, despite the fact that their relations had grown very warm, replacing the custodial posture Mrs D had adopted since her father's death. When it was suggested that this secretiveness must be part of a diffusely hurtful demeanour to her mother, the patient tried to establish that this was not the case. When her questions to her mother were answered by "Well I know you love me", Mrs D could not see the resignation implied. In fact the evidence all pointed in the direction of her having been a child of some sinew, with whom a technique of compromise had been early adopted. Her obstinacy was immense and could easily have been driven to self-destructive activity if not appeased. In addition she had held her little sister hostage in many ways. In the transference situation it was clear that her need to be "right" was an overriding passion and could be traced back with some conviction to the conjoint events of her second year: birth of the sister, moving out of the parental bedroom, and move to a new house.

The erotic relationship to the analyst as combined parents repeated in great detail the blissful period in the parents' bedroom and its attendant confusion of identity (Meltzer, 1967). It seemed clear from dreams that the year abroad in Canada had been similarly experienced in the depths so that the return to London had stirred recollections of the great expulsion, never forgiven. Her revenge on her parents in childhood had taken the form of arrogating to herself a very sanctimonious secrecy regarding her sexuality, which was meant to parallel the establishment of the privacy of their bedroom. She became a child who confided everything else as a screen for this breach of faith and, for a long time after the erotic transference subsided, this double standard of confidentiality reappeared in the analytic situation. But gradually her dreams gave away its content of a rather diffuse anal perversity. Its enactment in her marriage was revealed and a disengagement from it was slowly effected.

In consequence of this the analytical separations were felt more keenly and this made it possible for a clear delineation to be made between the adult part of her personality and infantile structures. These latter included a very dependent baby, urgently needing the "toilet-mummy" (Meltzer, 1967) but afraid of falling from the height of the feeding-breast; and in addition there appeared a know-it-all big sister part. This was the part that knew better than mummy and sat in harsh judgement on almost everyone. The one exception to this was seen to be her maternal grandmother, to whom the qualities of "parental" continued to have adhered historically. This was paralleled in the analysis by the status of Melanie Klein, while the analyst, like the parents, was felt to be highly sexual but of dubious reliability.

As we proceeded into the third year of the analysis Mrs D seemed to lapse into a desultory type of resistance to the work, bringing her material with a shrug and listening to interpretations with scarcely disguised boredom and misgivings about what seemed to her the analyst's cavalier attitude towards evidence. She explicitly considered as unworthy of respect a so-called science whose criteria of truth-function lay in the aesthetic realm, which proved nothing and could convince no-one. This reached hilarious proportions one day in an incident involving a cobweb hanging from the ceiling of the consulting room. Somehow the question arose as to its origin: did it necessarily imply a spider or were other events possible, such as particles of dust adhering by static electricity. Mrs D promptly looked it up, not in a physics or biology text but in the New Oxford Dictionary, and that was that. The possibility of my personal experience was ruled out in favour of definition. Whatever the analyst's experience of other phenomena might have been, they could not have been "cobwebs". He was making a linguistic error, playing the wrong "language-game" (Wittgenstein, 1953).

The debate about meaning and its relation to language came as climax to a series of dreams involving the patient's mother. Frequently the two of them were *climbing hills together, having picnics on cliffs overlooking the sea or were upstairs in a house preparing food.* In these many settings she was in continual conflict with her mother as to whose judgement was best. Her mother was endlessly patient, yielding and kind, while she was endlessly tolerant of mother's limited knowledge, her rigidity, her age and fatigue, provincial narrowness, etc. The problem of bringing this baby into a trusting dependence on the breast was clearly aggravated by the persistence of her infantile identity being invested in the "big sister" part. It seemed quite hopeless as she lay session after session treating the analytical method in this way, bored, playing with her beads, shrugging her baby-shoulders, marching off at the end of the session with her baby-nose in the air. But a dream gave promise of a chink in the armour.

Two months earlier she had had a dream which seemed to make reference to her dislike of the timbre of her own voice: *she discovered that the piano sounded so poorly because there was a weasel hiding in it, and producing a corrosive froth. But when she tried to put it out the window, it kept getting back inside despite the two big guard-dogs.* This seemed to link clearly with the acid contempt in her voice, with her eyes always ferreting out the defects and overlooking the virtues of the analyst. The way in which this operated to frustrate the breast in its attempts to fill the baby with something good and the way it was related to the perverse sexual trends found a brilliantly condensed representation in a very frightening and crucial dream with a rich associative framework. In the dream *it seemed that scripture was no longer to be taught in the schools in London as the children would not accept it unless it was called something high-flown like "moral philosophy". Then she seemed to be in a classroom where one girl was passing out pieces of cotton wool while another was making a mystic invocation to invite a giant bird to swoop down and carry off some other girl. At that moment a bird-woman appeared at the window, beating against the glass with her wings and a piece of wood. Mrs D felt terrified she would break in.*

The associations to the dream were revealing and poignant. When they had been in Canada, living in a cottage, a robin had come every morning and beat against the bedroom window. Mrs D thought it must have had a nest there when the cottage had stood unoccupied. On the day before the dream the patient had had to go to Oxford on business and had felt uneasy that she might see the analyst on the street there. But instead, to her dismay, on the way home she had seen her mother get off to change trains at Reading. She did not see or hear the patient call to her because Mrs D could not open the window. She realized that she could have had the pleasure of riding with her mother had not her omniscience prevented her phoning the cousin with whom mother was staying in Oxford, so certain had she been that mother's visit was to last longer.

It was unmistakable, therefore, that the bird-woman in the dream, like the robin in Canada, represented her mother trying to get back in touch with the good baby—who, however, was being made deaf to the truth (the cotton for the ears?) and dominated by the propaganda of the know-it-all séance-holding weasel-eyed "big sister". Theoretically this would represent an inability to effect a satisfactory splitting-and-idealization of self and object (Klein, 1932).

In the months that followed, an interesting and very gradual alteration in behaviour and mood took place in the consulting room. The shoulder-shrugging contempt for the psychoanalytical method and the spiteful scepticism about its efficacy, all based on her delusion-of-clarity-of-insight and sitting-in-judgement, changed to a brooding pessimism about herself and her character. She felt keenly the adamantine streak in herself and how it resisted being helped or being dependent—how it clung somehow by preference to the promise of perverse excitement, even though it no longer put this into action. She began to note similar qualities among some of the people she had previously admired, and to see how it wrecked their constructive aims and cost so much pain to the people who were fond of them. It was at first a harsh judgement on herself—one that would have passed sentence for punishment —but slowly this softened to sympathy and regret, even at times a bit remorseful, for the pain she inflicted on others and on herself. She felt herself to be a real "schizophrenogenic" mother and wondered at the flourishing of her children, who indeed did seem somehow to have benefited more from her analysis than she had herself. It was striking now how session after session she arrived in gloom and left cheerful. She insisted that this was just because I let her talk about her children and that was nice. Still she could recognize that the cheerfulness had something to do with the analyst's "foolish optimism" getting into her temporarily. She was even beginning to think there might be a beauty in the method that she could not see. But mainly her good feelings adhered to the analyst personally. It was he who could bear the weasel-eyes and the shoulder-shrugging. Perhaps some day she would shed the secrecy about her love and wear her heart on her sleeve. But it would have to be very slow; she was not a plunger-in.

Almost on the anniversary of the "bird-woman" dream another amused Mrs D and heartened the analyst, for in it a young lion was hurling himself at her windscreen and it seemed only a matter of time before he broke through. But later she was outside the car lifting a cat in her arms and closing some gate to keep a child from straying out of the garden. It was quite clear to her now that the delusion-of-clarity-of-insight came from being inside her object looking out of its eyes, and that the world—and the analysis—looked quite different from outside. The frightening lion-breast, like the bird-woman, became the attractive cat-breast that she could now take into herself as the basis of her own motherliness.

Summary

This short paper on the psychopathology of insight and judgement has set out to demonstrate one type of disturbance which can be seen to arise from the operation of the unconscious infantile phantasy of projective identification with the internal objects, especially the mother's breast and head, experienced as the fount of knowledge and wisdom. Fragments of material have been brought to illustrate the operation of the mechanism and then a more extensive description of an analysis was attempted. This latter sought to trace the relation of the patient's character pathology to a defensive structure which had been mounted in the second year of life under the pressure of disappointment and jealousy of the new baby sister. While in many ways the harshness and judgemental quality of the character was in the nature of a revenge against the parents for expelling her from a blissful confusion of identity with them, it was also a defence against ever being caught so unawares again. Thus her epistemophilic instinct and high intelligence were re-enforced by defensive as well as aggressive motives. In the transference it was necessary to work through the dissolution of the narcissistic organization illustrated best in the "bird-woman" dream. In order to do this a difficult countertransference problem of tolerating hopelessness and humiliation had to be faced, throwing light on the magnitude of the difficulties from which Mrs D's parents had retreated. It is difficult to see how parents, no matter how sterling, could have done otherwise.

The internal experience of these two mental acts, delusion-of-clarity-of-insight and sitting-in-judgement, seems to shade so subtly into their healthy counterparts, insight and judgement, that it is difficult to see how anything other than a widening of the field of introspection could distinguish them. Respect for the laws of evidence, attention to the quality of reasoning, soliciting the opinion of others in crucial matters and other safeguards may help. But such intellectual and social safety-measures also pay a price by throwing-away the possible moment of inspiration that seems to have no evidential links, to which the laws of logic find no application and which may seem unintelligible when communicated to others for advice. And since all nascent creativity may be based on the seizing of such moments, Kierkegaard's (1941) "leap in the dark", there comes a time when reliance on one's own introspection, forlornly, must be attempted.

CHAPTER SEVEN

Tyranny

Introduction by Irene Freeden

The chapter on "Tyranny" is the culmination of Meltzer's original thinking in his book *Sexual States of Mind*—a collection of lectures and papers set meticulously in a comprehensive structure. Its first part, "History", succinctly summarises the theories of Freud, Abraham and Klein on sexual development. Using them as a springboard, Meltzer offers his novel reading of Freud's theory of sexual psychopathology, a reading that insists on the crucial distinction between polymorphism and the perversity of infantile sexuality. The fundamental nature of that difference lies in its definition of the structure of the internal world.

The second part of the book, "Structural Revision of Sexual Theory", unfolds Meltzer's own view of psychosexual development. It emphasises infantile polymorphous sexuality as opposed to its perverse counterpart that tends to contaminate adult sexual life. "Dread, persecution and terror" (to reverse the original order) of the internal dead babies is the basis for his "structural revision of the theory of perversions and addictions" and their clinical manifestations in the "perversion of the transference". The clinical and metapsychological basis of Meltzer's future book on the Claustrum is beginning to emerge here.

Part Three of the book, "Application of theory", presents Meltzer's apparently tentative yet courageous attempt to allow psychoanalysis to make better sense of the state of the world and—through thinking about that world—to influence it. It contains chapters about healthy versus pathological relationships between generations, about enabling children's development through psychoanalytic insight, on abortion, and on the difference between art and pornography. "Tyranny" illustrates how Meltzer's psychoanalytical theory was deduced from his clinical exploration of internal tyrannical states in addictions and perversions. Meltzer fashions an analogy between the individual and the political: the persecuted/ persecutory internal individual world is the consequence of an attempt to avoid the pain and responsibility of the depressive position, while political tyranny is a "social perversion" that reaches its pinnacle in the obscenity of war. This chapter suggests a role that psychoanalysts, armed with their professional knowledge, could play in society at large. And perhaps, in the current state of the world, we can take serious note of its message of hope rooted in the psychoanalytic method.

Tyranny[i]
(1968)

This paper has undergone three stages of metamorphosis beginning in 1962 when a conjunction of several experiences—some clinical material, a piece of sculpture, and a jurist's memoirs—galvanised a paper read to the Imago Group. The second stage was the working out of a concept of terror and dread, which I consider a supplement to Dr Bion's

---

[i] First published in 1968, this paper is reprinted as Chapter 20 of Meltzer's *Sexual States of Mind* (1973), pp. 143-150.

theory of "nameless dread". This paper was read at the 1967 Congress.[i] The present stage is an amalgam and development which probes the social context of tyranny on the basis of psycho-analytical findings regarding internal tyranny in the perversions and addictions, but also aims to open the question of the social role of psycho-analysis, analysts and their societies in respect of these social phenomena.

Felix Frankfurter, the American jurist and Supreme Court justice, says in his talks with Harlen Phillips:

> I do take law very seriously, deeply seriously, because, fragile as reason is and limited as law is as the expression of the institutionalised medium of reason, that is all we have standing between us and the tyranny of mere will and the cruelty of unbridled undisciplined feeling. (Phillips 1960, p. 189)

This statement seems to me to epistomise the confusion between the law as explicit statement of the social contract, and law as the rules for excluding and punishing the pariah. I have met this conflict in patients again and again at the threshold of the depressive position when the coming of trust and dependence on good primal objects is still so confluent with possessive jealousy in regard to them that punishment—even extermination—of the split-off bad parts of the self, in their projected representations in the outside world, is demanded as a right, a reward of fealty, a precondition of continued trust.

As penetration into the depressive position deepens, the function of sitting-in-judgement is surrendered to the internal objects at infantile levels and with it, by introjection, there results an amelioration of the sanctimony. Who would not have been a Nazi in Hitler's Germany? Who can be sure, except the handful who stood the test? Otto Fenichel refers to Engel's description of the Peasant War of 1525 and derives from it a far more ego-defensive implication than Frankfurter's idea of law. He writes:

---
[i] "Terror, persecution and dread—a dissection of paranoid anxieties" (1967) is reprinted as Chapter 14, *Sexual States of Mind*, pp. 99-106.

In all wars, whether external or internal, there have been and are cruelties that are far in excess of tactical necessities and of the amounts of hatred actually mobilised in the single individual. Only psychology can explain these. Glover consider this to be a proof that deep-rooted instinctual drives are the true causes of wars, while what is ordinarily regarded as their causes were "rationalisation" of these destructive drives. One can disagree with Glover's view without denying the existence of biologically founded pleasure in cruelty. One of the problems is that at most diverse periods the cruelties of war assume very similar and quite definite forms, in particular cruelties inflicted in order to dishonour the adversary. These involve either a chopping off of limbs or cannibalistic acts, or symbolic allusions to them. For instance, to quote Engels ("The Peasant War in Germany", 1926): "Many prisoners were executed in the cruellest manner, the rest were sent home with nose and ears cut off... the peasants were attacked and dispersed by Zapolya; Dosa himself was taken prisoner, roasted on a red-hot throne and eaten alive by his own men, whose lives were spared solely on this condition...". Now, these atrocities were committed not by the rebels but by the representatives of law and order; and one often has the impression that in the history of the world such things have been done more often and more extensively by the defenders of the loyal state than by the insurgents. It can be established that roasting alive and eating a human being is not prescribed punishment in any judiciary system. What was the purpose of this cruel command? To scorn and humiliate a beaten foe. And what determines the form of this scorn and humiliation? What was once one's own longed-for instinctual aim, but later on succumbed to repression, is imposed on others in mockery and scorn.[i]

However, it is very evident that this imposition of the commitment of an instinctual, or perhaps paranoidal, crime is a far easier

---

[i] Extract from O. Fenichel, "Trophy and triumph", *International Review of Psycho-analysis*, Vol. 24 (3), 1939, pp. 258-80.

task than its converse—the imposition of the relinquishment of such crimes, on the one hand, or giving up of instinctual libidinal gratifications on the other. Amusing examples of the difficulty of western man in imposing such restrictions on the Marquesans and Tahitians respectively can be found in Herman Melville's lovely books *Typee* and *Omoo*.

Tyranny is not an expression of "mere will and the cruelty of unbridled, undisciplined feeling" but is a social perversion in defence against depressive anxieties. Furthermore, it is a social process for commerce in seemingly hopelessly mutilated internal objects. It grows out of cowardice in the face of the pains of the depressive position. The committing of tyranny engenders smugness and the submission to it generates apathy.

Clinical material

The first three years of analysis of a deeply schizoid young man had been occupied with the rehabilitation of the internal parents with whose severe mental and physical mutilations he had become intensely identified. Only a secret, bizarre manic omnipotence had saved him from total despair. From early childhood, his ego states had been of two kinds: those dominated by his feeling of being horribly disfigured and hopelessly mentally deficient, and those private withdrawn states in which he felt himself a unique genius or saint, a figure of overpowering beauty and endless creative potency. The first state rendered him incapable of socialization, partially ineducable, exquisitely sensitive to ridicule and helpless in the face of aggression. The latter state, in the sequestration of the family, brought forth a parade of delusional identities even as a small child: composer-pianist, commanding officer, news commentator, engine driver, and editor-in-chief. These, carried out with a brilliance of detailed observation and talent for mime, were hilarious enough to cause the family to overlook the delusional intensity with which they were being dramatised and the secret contempt in which the laughing adults were being held. In the complete isolation of his bed, a proliferation of masturbation into sado-masochistic perversions took place involving painful penetration of his various orifices.

The very uphill work of the first three years succeeded in sufficiently restoring the goodness and beauty of his internal mother and her breasts and the devotion and potency of the internal father and his genitals so that something resembling the analytic process began to take shape, with periods of co-operation, shattered by impending separations, and by negative therapeutic reactions following emergence of positive feelings whenever distance rumblings of depressive anxieties were followed by panicky retreats into omnipotence and schizoid indifference.

In this context, a monumental jealous of the next baby, linked to his two-years'-younger brother in the past, and to the prospect of the analyst undertaking new analytic cases, began to dominate the separation situations. During the fourth and fifth years of analytic work, mutilating attacks on the genitalia of the internal parents and on the babies inside the internal mother, occurred regularly in connection with holidays.

The autumn of the fifth year was occupied with two related types of behaviour about which he was very secretive. One was the drawing of pornographic pictures in connection with his masturbatory activities. The other was the evasion of physical proximity due to a delusion of smelling bad. This, he felt, was caused by a continual silent passage of flatus from an incontinent anus which he imagined he had damaged by his perversions. In the course of analysis, this latter problem began to alternate with outbreaks of vivacity and "passing jokes" at work and in the consulting room.

By the following February he had burned his pornography and toward the end of the month he was able to reveal that the pictures he drew showed women's bodies in various degrees of mutilation. That May he reported a dream in which *he was afraid of the incriminating evidence on a piece of paper and, with his penis, was pushing it into his sister's anus.* He felt puzzled in the dream as to why she was submitting to it.

This illustrates the patient's devices for ridding himself of the mutilated body—the *corpus delicti*—of his internal objects by expelling it into the split-off feminine part of himself, projected outside, as a defence against the pains of the depressive position. Since the mutilated objects were by various means projected into other persons in his unconscious phantasy, these persons were felt to be burdened by the feelings and responsibilities he evaded. Smugness resulted, for the damage was not visible to him within his own inner world. All feelings of guilt, grief, remorse, and longing, were obviated. A feeling of total helplessness about reparation pervaded all such depressive anxieties, and the victims of his projection of damaged objects were therefore felt to be burdened with this total life-sapping despair also. Every orifice of another person's body, including of course the eyes, could be utilised for this penetration. Any product of his own mind or body could become the carrier of the mutilated object.

During the analytic work of the second half of the sixth year, a process of integration began very slowly to take place as a result of the gradually increasing desire to protect and preserve the beautiful internal mother, the analyst, and his external mother. The analyst and his mother represented the two people in the outside world who were linked to his good internal object. It was a split-off part of the patient's personality that had originally inflicted the mutilations on his internal world. This part, because of its grinding relentlessness of destructive activity, had at first been represented in dreams only as machines—tanks, battleships etc. Through the fifth and sixth years it had been represented in dreams and extensive acting-out by a cat, "Tigger", and it came to be known to us as the "Tigger-part" of the patient. By the autumn of the sixth year, there was occasional representation of this part in human form in his dreams, and its activities slowly began to reach consciousness. Earlier, they had been bound in the delusion of continual passage of flatus. Now they became manifest as a continual whispering on the couch whenever the analyst was interpreting: a whispering of cynical, ridiculing and abusive refutation of the interpretation.

The approach to the Christmas break of the sixth year was unusually successful in preserving the good internal mother and thus good feelings and hope in the analysis. Extreme anxiety about the analyst's safety and a deep misery of loneliness began to emerge into consciousness. In the last session before the break, he presented a dream in which *he saw a disreputable-looking negro asleep in a ditch in the rain. He woke him up, and the fellow then followed him as he went downhill, all the while pressing his penis against the patient's buttocks.* The dream shows clearly that the destructive and now hated part of himself had been temporarily put at rest until the patient awakened its cruelty. It reveals that he was going downhill of his own accord—no-one was forcing him. He wished to regress, to escape the loneliness, the anxiety of any depressive pain. The dream links with the one of his sister.

In February of the next year, after a very difficult struggle to restore the ground lost in his collapse over Christmas, he dreamed —after an analytic hour preoccupied with Eichmann and the Nazi extermination camps—that *there was a group of people of three generations outside the analyst's consulting room. They were shabby and starved, but singing and dancing with mixed gaiety and sadness. A young woman tried to take his hand and draw him into the group, but he pulled away and walked downhill. Then he was in his room, looking at himself naked in the mirror. He could not see his penis, but as he lifted his leg he was horrified to see that there was a third leg behind it.*

I interpreted, and he agreed, that he was horrified to discover that he had walked downhill with Eichmann behind him, as in the "negro" dream, allowing him to make an extermination camp of his inner world. He was confronted with the choice of joining the human family—the "three generations"—where sadness and gaiety are mixed; or joining the Nazis who hate and intend to exterminate all loving bonds among people. He chose the latter, by allowing the Eichmann part of himself to exterminate his good internal objects—that is, to destroy the basis of his capacity to love objects in the outside world, to feel himself part of the human family, to be concerned with the welfare of others. It is vital to note, however, that when he pulled himself away from the young woman who was trying to catch his hand, he did so to avoid the pains represented by the shabby and starved appearance of the group and the pathos of their entertainment. When he realised that by doing so he had given Eichmann dominion over his inner world and thereby sacrificed his self-esteem, represented by his penis, he was horrified.

This material was very vivid in my mind when I saw Ralph Brown's "Two Figures with a Carcass" exhibited at Battersea. It powerfully integrates the formal and emotional aspects of this material. My view at that time was expressed in the dialogue with Adrian Stokes published in *Painting and the Inner World*,[i] and was, I now think, a pessimistic one as regards the social role of psychoanalysis and analysts. It tended to shift the entire burden to artists—or rather the "art world"—of carrying on the social equivalent of the psychoanalytical method of interpretation with a view to lessening of paranoid anxieties and strengthening the bonds of relationship to good objects by which greater capacities for depressive pain might develop. Its hope was that the findings of psychoanalysis might percolate through the "art world", especially through the analytic treatment of artists. It might be said to have left the field to humanism as the heir to the church.

The hopefulness about the particular patient described above and in my 1963 paper on "Somatic Delusions" did not find confirmation in subsequent years' work, for his progress ground to a halt and has not yet been re-established. However, the problem which I could not penetrate with him was revealed and worked through with other patients, and was reported in my 1967 paper on "Terror, persecution, and dread" [*op.cit*]. Its findings were summarised as follows:

> Terror is a paranoid anxiety whose essential quality paralysis, leaves no avenue of action. The object of terror, being in unconscious phantasy dead objects, cannot even be fled from with success. But in psychic reality the vitality of an object, of which it may be robbed, can also be returned to it, as the soul to the body in theological terms. This can only be accomplished by the reparative capacity of the internal parents and their creative coitus.

---

[i] Meltzer & Stokes, "Concerning the social basis of art" (1963), reprinted in Meltzer & Williams, *The Apprehension of Beauty* (1988), pp. 206-26.

When dependence on the reparative capacity of the internal objects is prevented by oedipal jealousy and/or destructive envy, this restoration cannot occur during the course of sleep and dreaming. Only an object in external reality, which bears the transference significance of the mother's breast at infantile levels, can accomplish the task. This may be undertaken innumerable times without being acknowledged, if the infantile dependence is blocked by the denigrating envy or the obstinacy born of intolerance to separation.

Where dependence on good internal objects is rendered infeasible by damaging masturbatory attacks and where dependence on a good external object is unavailable or not acknowledged, the addictive relationship to a bad part of the self—the submission to tyranny—takes place. An illusion of safety is promulgated by the omniscience of the destructive part and perpetuated by the sense of omnipotence generated by the perversion or addictive activity involved. The tyrannical, addictive, bad part is *dreaded*. It is important to note that while the tyrant may behave in a way that has a resemblance to a persecutor—especially if any sign of rebellion is at hand—the essential hold over the submissive part of the self is by way of the *dread of loss of protection against the terror*. I have come to the conclusion that intolerance to depressive anxieties *alone* will not produce the addictive constellation of submission to the tyrant, nor in combination with persecution by the damaged object. Where a dread of loss of an addictive relation to a tyrant is found in psychic structure, the problem of terror will be found at its core, as the force behind the dread and the submission.

Until such narcissistic organisation is dismantled and a rebellion against tyranny of the bad part is mounted, progress into the threshold of the depressive position is impossible. Furthermore, until this occurs, factors in psychopathology such as intolerance to separation, or to depressive pain, or cowardice in the face of persecution, cannot be accurately estimated. The dread felt in relation to the tyrant is fundamentally a dread of loss of the illusory protection against the terror and may be seen to appear especially at times when rebellion has been undertaken in alliance with good objects which are then felt to be inadequate or unavailable, as during analytic holiday breaks.

In this summary I had not stressed a point concerning which I have grown increasingly convinced in the two years since its writing: namely, that in the final analysis, these "dead objects" are the internal mother's inside babies.

Summary and discussion

I have now presented an account of the development of my views over the six years 1962-68 on the subject of tyranny as a social phenomenon and have chosen to do so here in this way, because I feel that the call to action is altered and that the capitulation to humanism with its common sense can be reversed. Psychoanalysis is, I am convinced, the antithesis of common sense just as cynicism is its perversion, since it considers the laws of psychic reality, not external reality, to be primary. While common sense may appeal against cynicism in respect of enlightened self-interest, it can never plead within the depressive position without appearing weak and sentimental. It is bound to egocentricity, when all is said and done. It cannot conceive a realm of mind that is beyond self, as Freud has taught us to do with his discovery of the concreteness of the super-ego. Psychoanalysts are therefore equipped with a theory, and with a method of using it, which can see meaning in human actions in dimensions of time and depth not available to common sense, nor to introspection short of the prophetic.

The theory of tyranny engenders foresight, and foresight makes action possible. The essence of this foresight is to be able to recognise in the outside world actions which are bound to have the meaning in psychic reality of the murdering of the internal mother's inside babies, where the paradigm of war and the concentration camp fails us in their delineation, and common sense gives tacit approval. Shall I mention some areas of social debate where psychoanalytical thought is required? The fisheries, methods of contraception, organ transplant, wild life conservation, divorce, drug taking, factory farming, vivisection afforestation, archaeology, criminal law and penology, mortuary practices, safeguarding of libraries and museums, zoos, marriage, abortion, pollution.

May it not be that the tyranny and the ultimate perversion, war, is forced upon us by accumulations of unconscious terror and depressive anxiety constantly generated by activities which appear innocent to common sense, where we "know not what we do?" Perhaps only psychoanalysts have the method and material to delineate these areas and expose these activities.

CHAPTER EIGHT

Dimensionality, adhesive identification, splitting

Introduction by Renata Li Causi

Explorations in Autism contains the case histories of four autistic children, treated by psychotherapists trained in Melanie Klein's psychoanalytic model of child therapy and closely supervised by Meltzer. By the end of this research the book has formulated a new way of thinking about this syndrome, with significant further implications.

Meltzer noticed that autistic children experience an object with only one sense at a time (an object is seen, or heard, or touched, etc.). This provides an early defence against painful or intense emotions, earlier than splitting, which he calls "dismantling". They let their mental organization fall passively to pieces, resulting in a state of mindlessness which has devastating consequences for their growth. Autistic children fail to form three-dimensional concepts of objects which contain spaces, and their concept of time is also severely impaired; they cannot identify either projectively or introjectively. Their perception is of an object without an inside (bidimensional objects). The alternative identification which they create is of skin-to-skin contact, which was called by Mrs Bick "adhesive identification". Bick demonstrated the need for the experience of a containing object before primal splitting-and-idealization (Klein) could take place. Meltzer says, on the strength of the clinical material presented here, that autistic children have either lost or never developed an adequate psychic skin. His description of these children's defective psychic skin is not quite the same as the phenomenon described by Bick, as it seems to be the result of deficient concept formation rather than of inadequate containment under stress and anxiety.

Ten years later, writing *The Apprehension of Beauty*, Meltzer made an important addition to his formulation about autism—the idea that the beauty of the objects had an unbearable impact on the autistic child, as he felt bombarded by the sensory experience of the "ordinary beautiful mother".

Dismantling, employment of mindlessness, impairment of spatial and temporal concepts are observable in ordinary and ill people alike. These formulations are invaluable in thinking about highly disturbed patients, omnipotent and destructive, where the concepts of narcissistic organization, minute splitting mechanisms, interpretation of attacks on the objects do not seem to describe fully, or usefully, their experience. Basic mental functions have been attacked, or lost, or perhaps never developed.

Three-dimensionality[i]
(1975)

Once the object has been experienced as resisting penetration, so that the emotional problems no longer seem merely ones of being on one side or the other of a paper-thin object (front-side and back-side for instance), the stage is set [...] for the conception to arise of orifices in object and

---

i Extract from Meltzer, Chapter 9 in Meltzer, Bremner, Hoxter, Weddell & Wittenberg, *Explorations in Autism* (1975), pp. 226-27.

self. The struggle can then commence concerning the guarding or closing of these orifices, which are conceived as natural rather than forced or torn. With the inception of this new struggle the entire view-of-the-world rises to a new level of complexity, the three-dimensional one, of objects and, by identification, the self, as containing potential spaces.

The potentiality of a space, and thus the potentiality of a container, can only be realized once a sphincter-function has become effective. It is with the evolution and development of these sphincters that so much of Barry's analysis was concerned. His material shows with particular clarity that the capacity of the object to protect and thus to control its own orifices is a precondition for the self to make a move in that direction, of continence as well as of resistance to aggressive penetration.

But insofar as the inside of an object also persists in having the meaning of a prior state of mind—for the feeling of being adequately contained is a precondition for the experience of being a continent container—the movements in phantasy of getting into and out of an object necessarily have a significance with regard to the conception of time. Time which had been indistinguishable from distance in the one-dimensional mindlessness and had achieved a certain vague continuity or circularity from moving from point to point on the surface of a two-dimensional world, now begins to take on a directional tendency of its own, a relentless movement from inside to outside the object.

But the continued operation of omnipotence fashions the phantasy of projective identification. By this means not only is there asserted the reversibility of differentiation of self from object but also, as a corollary, a claim is put forward concerning the reversibility of the direction of time.

Oscillatory time thus arises in the mind's conceptions of "the world" and must wait upon the painful, and never fully completed, movement of relinquishment of projective identification in order to become one-directional. Time then becomes the implacable spouse of Fate, that imponderable random factor in the outside world.

Adhesive identification in neurotic and psychotic patients[i]

I have quoted at length from Mrs Bick's paper ["The experience of the skin in early object relations"] because it not only delineates the probem of the skin-container function and its relation to ego strength but also goes some distance to sorting out the methods by which this ego strength can be simulated in what she calls a "second-skin" function. I have earlier described some of the findings with the children of this study which illustrate the various aspects of impaired mental function which we thik are contingent upon the failure to achieve three-dimensionality in the conception of self and object which is the necessary pre-condition to the container-function. Where Mrs Bick has demonstrated a step in mental organization of experience proximal in time to the operation of splitting-and-idealization (which in turn is preconditional to splitting-and-projective-identification), we are attempting a further step. Instead of defects in the container-function of the object we are attempting to describe defects in the conception-of-the-object as container, namely the two-dimensional conception. Clinical experience of neurotic and psychotic patients enables us to amplify these descriptions by another phenomenon which is linked on the one hand to preoccupation with surface phenomena between self and objects, and on the other hand to the impairment of time sense resulting from a failure to conceive of enduring change—circular time.

Splitting and L,H,K[ii]

There have been only two compelling addenda to Freud's conception of mental life's commencement in the baby, namely his idea of primary narcissism as a state in which identification with satisfying objects was immediate, automatic. These amplifications were, in the first instance, Melanie Klein's

---

[i] Extract from Chapter 9, *Explorations in Autism*, pp. 234-35.
[ii] Extract from Chapter 10, *Explorations in Autism*, pp. 239-43.

description of the primal splitting-and-idealization of self and object, originally the breast (meaning the mother as breast). By this operation the child laid the foundations for concepts of good and bad, albeit grossly exaggerated and immediate in criteria. This was considered by Melanie Klein to mark the commencement of object relations conducive to healthy development, a sine qua non. The second corollary was added by Esther Bick in 1968 with her description of the psychic function of the skin in mental development. She convincingly demonstrated the need for an experience of a containing object with which the baby can be identified in order to feel sufficiently contained within its own skin to be able to bear being put down by the mother in a waking state without disintegration of the body-self. She traced some of the consequences for ego-strength of a defective psychic skin and showed how substitute, second-skin functions are established to bolster the defect. Bick saw this as a prerequisite to adequate splitting-and-idealization, and therefore to the satisfactory resolution of good-bad confusions.

The massive material of the clinical chapters of this book declares unequivocally that we are dealing with children in whom both these steps in development were either lost or inadequate to begin with. But we do not find the usual proliferation of persecutory anxieties, paranoid suspicions and sadistic perversity. On the contrary, the children are gentle, tender, easily cast into despairing depression, more irritated than frightened by their omnipresent rival-babies. It is only after the analysis and development has proceeded a certain distance that narcissistic hardness and cruelty with consequent persecutory fears and paranoid suspicion makes its appearance in Timmie or John. Even Barry is very little frightened of persecutors but rather is persecuted by the depressive feelings engendered by his continual damage to his object from brutal intrusiveness (the holiday bandaging for instance) and did not develop a narcissistic organization until after the establishment of an internal world and the splitting-and-idealization of self and objects ("now I know why I am ugly") [...] On the road to improved structure the children became more manifestly cruel and hard as splitting-and-idealization made narcissistic organization possible.

Now there is some sort of lesson hidden in these findings, something having to do with splitting-and-idealization, of good and evil as mental categories, something that raises a question about their necessity. The charge that Milton made Satan the hero of *Paradise Lost* is perhaps not without substance, for not many men can be seen to have struggled as Milton did to contain and deal personally, responsibly, with every aspect of himself *vis à vis* his object, God. It is clear that Melanie Klein viewed splitting processes as being instituted violently, by destructive impulses, regardless of the purpose or motive behind their deployment. The consequence of splitting was seen by her as always damaging to the object to some degree and therefore an occasion of guilt and remorse. And it is true, as we study splitting processes, they do have the quality of a judgment handed down and executed, regardless of the wisdom of Solomon that may lie behind it.

But it is also perhaps true that splitting processes are necessary for the kind of decisions that make action in the outside world possible. Every decision involves the setting in motion of a single plan from amongst its alternatives; it is experimental, involves risk, a certain ruthlessness towards oneself or others. I remember as a schoolboy being shown a science film on crystallography dealing with the cutting of a huge rough diamond of very great value. The cutters studied its structure, drew lines of its presumptive natural cleavages, and then, at the moment of great suspense, applied a little chisel, gave it a tiny tap, and the diamond fell into two clean parts. I was greatly impressed. But I am also greatly impressed by the fourteen-year-old Piffie's dream of a precious object that has natural lines of cleavage. While Mrs Bick may have discovered the secret of ego-strength, Piffie has perhaps discovered the secret of ego-resilience, of stooping-to-conquer, the reeds that bend while the oak goes down before the gale. In a word, temporizing by disengagement.

Temporizing immediately raises the spectre of hesitation, indecision, procrastination, compromise, hallmark of the obsessional character. Where does the difference lie? In what way is Piffie's obsessionality different from that of Freud's "Rat Man"? One clear answer is that Freud's patient deployed his obsessional separating and controlling in the interest of his ambivalence to his "lady", his love and hate. Piffie's obsessionality does not serve his ambivalence, which is in fact very little in evidence. Truly his omnipotent control is meant to subserve his desire to possess his "Mrs Hoxter" just as completely as John wants his "lady", but through understanding of her inner workings, not force, ultimately. Like Barry's Mr McGoo, Piffie is a lover and wishes to understand his object so well that he can make it so blissful that it will not need, or want, other babies or daddy-penises. A primitive form of love? Yes. Egocentric? Yes. But authentic!

I must pause at this moment to pay heed to a phenomenon not infrequent in my scientific wanderings on the ice-cap. Whenever I approach a new landmark, I find on it a small cache of rocks and a little flag with the letter "B", for Bion, presumably. You will have noted that we have come round to the vertices L, H, and K: love, hate and knowledge. In Bionese I seem to be suggesting that the difference between Piffie and the Rat Man is one of vertices to their obsessionality: L and H for the Rat Man, K for Piffie. Thus we find that the lover, the artist and the scientist are the same person and that science can start very early. But it can also outgrow its source and proliferate as an illness. This would also imply the possibility of its not doing so, and of a type of healthy, resilient personality structure being erected by means not involving splitting-and-idealization. From this viewpoint the concepts of good and evil would not be necessary in the way described by Money-Kyrle in his investigation of the internal logic of development of the mind. I would also point out that this inquiry takes us back to Melanie Klein's early emphasis on the epistemophilic instinct as a driving force in development and the mother's body as the original "world" it explored.

This opens a window on the psychoanalytical method as a thing-in-itself that people can participate in, sometimes as the patient, sometimes as the analyst, eventually as both simultaneously. What is the emotionality stirred by this sort of experience? If the process is one dominated by the vertex of K, its essential events will be ones of becoming both knowing and known—something perhaps more Quixotic than Freud's self-appellation of "conquistador". But essentially the process would seem to deserve the name "adventure" and, at moments of fruition, would seem most appropriately accompanied—no not accompanied, suffused —suffused with the feeling of wonder at the beauty of the world of the mind, the only world we can really "know".

CHAPTER NINE

The impact of Bion's ideas

Introduction by Meg Harris Williams

This chapter represents Meltzer's summing-up in *Studies in Extended Metapsychology* of Bion's impact on him personally over the previous decades. By contrast with *The Kleinian Development*. which was primarily theoretical in content, this book explores a spectrum of clinical cases presented by colleagues, as well as some of his own, and considers the ways in which Bion's formulations illuminate further than the previously existing models our understanding of both the psychoanalytic process and a variety of clinical problems, as well as some implications of Bion's thinking for psychoanalysis generally.

The diverse areas that thereby come into focus include: the nature of language and symbol-formation in childhood and in the analytic situation; ways in which symbol-formation may be averted or perverted; the distinction between communicative projective identification and the intrusive identification which makes a container into a "claustrum"; types of self-deception, and a consideration of lies as a reversal of alpha-function; the potential of an awareness of the Negative Grid for sustaining the analyst in the fight against perversity; speculations about prenatal and "invertebrate" personality structure and its relation to psychotic illness in early childhood and to evaluating psychosomatic states; the caesura between protomental and mental, and how their interplay constantly "competes for the soul of the child"; the social elaboration of this in terms of psychoanalytic group politics, and the role of "magic" and "irritability" in such hierarchical settings.

In particular Meltzer homes in on something just touched on in *The Kleinian Development* and to be further developed in *The Apprehension of Beauty*—namely aesthetic experience as the key to mental development. A new view of psychoanalysis emerges in which the process itself is seen as the ultimate aesthetic or containing object for both patient and analyst. The primary task is to enable toleration of the psychic reality of the object, in the recognition that in the Bionic model, pleasure-pain payments are "fictitious" and instead, "development is happiness".

The impact of Bion's ideas[i]
(1986)

This sort of book, which is the residue of clinical and teaching experiences rather than of any systematic research, seems a kind of compost heap. It is primarily intended to increase the fertility of the next developmental steps of others, to help them to bring to life their nascent creativity. But one also tends to hope that something alive of one's own may be found, unexpectedly, to be growing on the heap—a clump of mushrooms or a surprise of daffodils. Does the book add up to anything other than what it claims: a series of studies illustrating the use that Bion's ideas have found in my consulting room?

Bion himself was very opposed to a distinct "school" growing up around his ideas, perhaps partly because the adjective "Bionic"

---

[i] "Denouement", Chapter 28 of Meltzer's *Studies in Extended Metapsychology: Clinical Applications of Bion's Ideas* (1986). pp. 203-11.

had such comic overtones of science fiction, gardening, electronics and quackery. But chiefly he felt, and I feel perhaps even more strongly, that the formation of "schools" is a miscarriage of science. It is naïve to suppose that deep and significant differences exist. It is political to exploit them within the organisations of psychoanalysis. It fails to understand the impossible task of rendering in language the ineffable phenomena of the mind. And finally it shows little comprehension of the history of art and science. In so far as the metaphor of progress as forward movement is permissible, the development of art and science—or in the case of psychoanalysis, art-science—moves forward in spiral fashion in some respects, or like a caterpillar in others. Those in the vanguard of development think they are miles ahead of the rearguard when they reckon linearly, but they need only look sideways to see that they are only inches in advance. Furthermore it is necessary for them to pause, and teach, and help the others to catch up before they can go on. If they fail to do this, their language—and soon their thoughtbecomes so idiosyncratic that they find they have departed from the social field and must find their way back. In a way this happened to Bion with *Transformations* and had to be rectified by altering his metaphors in *Attention and Interpretation*.

This process of catching up tends to be misunderstood in the context of school-formation and politics as if it were some sort of clandestine plagiarism, stealing ideas and couching them in different terminology. An example of this can be seen in the development of "self-psychology" around the work of Heinz Kohut with its strong reverberation of Kleinian notions. But closer examination shows that two other processes are at work: one of these is the refinement of the language of the vanguard to fasten it more firmly to its historic roots; the other is a watering-down of the concepts to achieve a greater respectability. Both of these have their value for the social structure of the psychoanalytical movement and its relations to the surrounding intellectual and scientific community. Neither of them inhibit further forward movement in the next wave of advance.

In viewing my own work as "exploration", I like to think that some attempt should be made to trace in a more personal way what

I see as the impact of Bion's ideas on my mode of life and view of the world (model of the mind, structure of history, evolution of political organisations, the role of the artist in the community, the nature of psychoanalysis as a thing, etc.).

In terms of Bion's concept of "catastrophic change" and the impact of the "new idea" there is no difficulty in establishing what this idea was and the revolution it has wrought in my ways of thinking and working… and also acting in general. The "new idea" was clearly something like: "In the beginning was the aesthetic object, and the aesthetic object was the breast and the breast was the world". Of course I am using the word "breast" as a technical term with only an implication of description, rather than the other way round. On the one hand it seems surprising to me that this idea did not reach me through Adrian Stokes to whom it was ever vivid; on the other hand it is difficult to say whence in Bion's work it derives. It is not in the Grid; it is only hinted at in *Transformations*; it tags along in a secondary position in *Attention and Interpretation*. Only in *A Memoir of the Future* does it find its place unambiguously. But it had reached me through Bion before that publication had crept into my thought and certainly into my consulting room. Not only had I become aware that the psychoanalytical method had taken on an aesthetic quality in my eyes but I had begun to see, mainly through dreams, that it had done so for some of my patients as well.

In retrospect I think the work on autism with its elaboration of the concept of dimensionality played an important role; the fine aesthetic sensibility of many of these children was so unmistakeable that one could not avoid wondering if their developmental failure had not been funded on processes for warding off the impact of the beauty of the world. Dismantling of the senses and two-dimensionality seemed exquisitely delicate methods for doing so without violence to the object, either externally or internally. The process of dismantling of the senses was too massive, too much like soul-murder, however, to illuminate the problem. But two-dimensionality held fascinating questions in its grip. At first it seemed that this shallowing of the world of meaning was self-explanatory, as if the dilution of meaning naturally resulted in an impoverishment of affects. Bion's ideas suggested the reverse: that a method of curtailing the intensity of affects resulted in the pallor of meaning. If this was the case, then the two-dimensional orientation to the world would be a defence against the impact of objects stirring emotions. But how? Melanie Klein's idea had been that interest in the inside of the mother, and thereby the epistemophilic instinct in general, had its origins in the intense emotionality of the mother-baby relationship. Did two-dimensionality then result from a denial of the psychic reality of the object rather than a regression to a prior stage in cognitive development?

Similarly old assumptions, tied up with Melanie Klein's delineation of paranoid-schizoid and depressive positions, were called into question. Esther Bick had revealed the identificatory processes connected with two-dimensionality (adhesive identification) so that it was feasible to think that an organisation of mentality prior to the paranoid-schizoid position might exist which would strengthen the assumption of a genetic sequence with a strong internal logic, placing the depressive position at a more sophisticated level of experience. But somehow Melanie Klein's formulation of the factors operating to set the epistemophilic instinct in motion did not seem to be satisfactory. Her failure to differentiate between intrusive curiosity and thirst for knowledge as factors in the little child's interest in the inside of the mother's body, weakened the conceptual fabric. Findings with autistic children suggested strongly that sadism and splitting processes were not intensely operative in their illness but only developed in force in the process of recovery and advance in development.

Dissatisfaction of this sort with the mind-model which operated in the consulting room must gradually have influenced a shift away from thinking in terms of genetic phases of development towards a field conception. The implicit complexity seemed to demand it. I remembered Melanie Klein saying in response to critics at a meeting that it was not she who made things complicated—they just were so. Of course the human mind must be the most complicated thing in the universe within our ken. And there must be a limit to the degree to which the mind, studying itself, can penetrate its mysteries. Perhaps mystery itself is an important aspect of its essence.

Bion's emphasis on consciousness, not as a system but as an organ of the mind—the organ of attention—had already been strongly recommended by the experiences with autistic children. Their diffusion of attention with its resulting dismantling of what Bion had, half-jokingly, called "common sense" (Sullivan's [1953] "consensuality") seemed at once a powerful and yet delicately sparing way of evading the impact of life both around and within themselves. The therapeutic indication of the importance of seizing and holding their attention with interesting talk based on acute observations, had demonstrated its efficacy, if also its tendency to exhaust the therapist.

The "field" orientation which accepts multiple levels of simultaneous and more-or-less integrated functioning seems to allow the question "how" and not only "when" is the mental level called into operation to superimpose itself on the purely neurophysiological? Bion's approach to the problem, by assuming that the first operation is the creation of thoughts which then require an apparatus to think (manipulate, use) them, seems to be the crucial break with the traditional implication that thinking is prior as a function and generates thoughts. It enabled him to create the Grid and then to move on to examine the "transformations" by which thinking implements its utilisation of thoughts. More than that, it provided a framework for considering false thoughts lies, misunderstandings, un-truth, misconceptions propaganda, cynicism. When this is compounded with the great step of opposing emotion to anti-emotion (positive and negative L, H and K) a new abacus lies to hand for thinking about thinking.

To be able to think of the mental as a "level" and of its being "called into play" by the focusing of attention on the emotionality being aroused by an experience, delivers a new freedom to our consideration of the problem. And it is not merely the semantic clarification that freshens the atmosphere, for it also sweeps away the traditional primary preoccupation with logic and thereby mathematics and linguistics as our supreme source of information, from the Greeks to the *Tractatus* [Wittgenstein 1922]. The "empty" concept of alpha-function is our new key. But the lock that it fits has also shifted; this is the crucial matter. We have been misled by confusing the creation of aesthetic objects as the work of rare and evolved genius with the perception of the beauty-of-the-world which Wordsworth asserted was inherent in the "clouds of glory" embodied in the mentality of children and their availability to the "splendour in the grass" ["Immortality Ode"]. Had he pursued the problem of the loss of this sensibility rather than accepting the facile explanation, essentially sociological, that "getting and spending we lay waste our powers", he would have recognised more clearly the nature of the pain that these sensibilities bring in their train.

Similarly Melanie Klein's loyalty to Freud's formulation of the duality of instinct caused her simply to by-pass the problem and explain away the evident ambivalence implicit in the epistemophilic instinct on the basis of frustration. This attitude is a bit surprising, considering that she knew very well that a certain optimal level of mental pain (frustration, persecution, envy, etc.) is necessary, since development is driven by tolerable conflict. My own first glimpse of the problem was recorded in a paper called "The Apprehension of Beauty", where I also failed to grasp what I had glimpsed, as I think had Hanna Segal [1952] in her famous paper on aesthetics.

And so they came together: the key of alpha-function and the lock of two-dimensionality: the enigma of the inside and the outside of the aesthetic object. Its power to evoke emotionality was only equalled by its ability to generate anxiety, doubt, distrust. While the sensuous qualities of the aesthetic object could be apprehended with some degree of confidence, its internal qualities—being infra- or supra-sensuous—carried no such comfort. Here observation needed to be coupled with thought and judgement, and judgement depended greatly for its firmness on experience. For it was in the matching or disparity of this outside and inside of the object of awe and wonder that its value for good or evil must surely reside. But the baby's experience of the world is almost nil. How is it to exercise such judgement? It cannot; it can only wait to see what will happen next.

This then would be the context in which absence of the object makes its crucial impact and tests the mettle. Bion [1965] has defined this problem of the absent object as "the absent object as a present persecutor" with respect to "the space where the object used to be", perhaps also by implication including Berkeley's "ghosts of departed quantities" [Bion 1991]. These "times that try men's souls"and find out the "summer soldier" in the depths[1] must be infinitely more stressful for the baby when we remember their impact on Othello and Leontes, and "La Belle Dame Sans Merci" [Keats]. Trust would then be a compound quality of mind, like foot-pounds as a definition of work: hope-hours, or minutes or days or years. In the very young it can at times seem more to be hope-seconds as the baby's face crumples when mother turns the corner out of sight.

By defining the fundamental problem of aesthetic relations in this way and by asserting the aesthetic relationship to the world as the primal stimulus to thought, we have adopted a position compatible with a field theory that is also inherently genetic. What it does, that the differentiation of paranoid-schizoid and depressive positions fails to do in their adherence to a Life and Death Instinct foundation, is to allow for a purely mental approach to values unencumbered by biological speculation. While the issue of mental pain and tolerance thereof loses none of its clinical vibrance as an arbiter of ego strength, a new factor is introduced to the dynamism of conflict. Trust, in units of hope-time, schematically speaking, would seem to have qualitative roots in the richness of the aesthetic experience to which separation is the sequel. And this richness is surely to be found in the element of mutuality of apprehension of beauty. For the baby must be held as an aesthetic object by the mother for the experience of their love-making to reverberate and escalate in intensity.

Such a basis which allows us to conceive the "how" of the calling into action of the capacity for symbolic thought, the product of the mysterious alpha-function, more or less releases us from any great concern with the "when" of the matter. Pre-natal or post-natal, it must occur. And if this conjunction of mutuality is its essential ingredient, its inception may be widely variable in time. But, sadly, we must recognise that it may not occur at all, as in the children who do not seem to make the post-natal adjustment or whose neurophysiological apparatus is not of sufficient complexity to achieve the aesthetic level of response. The autist and the non-developer may taste it and rebel against its dominance.

But more important for clinical practice is the corollary—that the defensive operations which psychoanalysis is specially fashioned to follow may mostly, perhaps entirely, be seen as moves against the impact of the aesthetic object, although this is not apparent in the early days of an analysis. It comes, in my view, at the threshold of the depressive position, after confusions have been sorted out. How then does this view essentially differ from Melanie Klein's formulations, and what precisely are the alterations in the consulting room which are generated by it?

Undoubtedly the first and most important alteration is a diminished emphasis on the "correctness" of interpretation, perhaps a lessening of the urgency to interpret altogether. Instead the focus moves forwards, as it were, into the interaction—the relationship from which interpretive ideas emerge. The model of container-contained places a new value on receptiveness and the holding of the dynamic situation of transference-countertransference in the mind. But perhaps to state this as if the analyst were the container misses the point that it is the fitting together of the analyst's attention and attitudes to the co-operativeness of the patient that forms and seals the container, lending it the degree of flexibility and resilience required from moment to moment.

Interpretation therefore loses its explanatory function, partly from the altered nature of the situation but also because the analyst has lost his causal orientation to mental events. The field of mental states will not allow the language of linearity to assert itself, falling away in favour of attempts at description, hopelessly inadequate in a sense, as a painting would be useless as a basis for botanical research. Instead the metaphor of illumination replaces explanation. I well remember visiting a cave in the Dordogne— Combarelles I think—full of engravings of ice-age animals. As the guide moved his lamp about from one angle to another, different superimposed images sprang from the wall.

The image of the analyst's verbal task—to shine a light of understanding from one vertex after another—modifies the atmosphere of communication to an extraordinary degree, diminishing the authoritarian expectations of the patient and sharing the responsibility between the members of the Work Group of two. It also allows an interpretive line gradually to form. Certain dreams—the dreams and not their interpretations—establish the landmarks for both members. The function of understanding, with all its uncertainty and readiness to yield its place, by divesting the analyst of the expectation of knowing, allows him far greater freedom of speculation. Intuitions for which the evidence is not as yet obtrusive can freely be given, the degree of uncertainty being indicated by the music of the voice. Since the mystification of seeming omniscience is thus stripped from the relationship, the patient becomes more interested in the method and welcomes explanation of the rationale of the analyst's behaviour. All this, including the improved definition of the shape which the psychoanalytic process seems to be assuming, tends to erect the concept of the science, the process, the method—taken together perhaps with its personal and institutional history—as a thing-in-itself that can, eventually, be apprehended as an aesthetic object.

This has far-reaching implications for the transference and countertransference, for it establishes an object upon which are not imposed (in Freud's terms) the limitations inherent in the "particularities" of the analyst—his age, sex, appearance, known facts about his life situation, his values, politics, etc. In fact it allows for the formation of an object which the therapist and patient can examine together from a certain distance, in the same way that one steps back from most paintings to allow the composition to impinge, and then steps forward to appreciate the brush strokes and craftsmanship.

Psychoanalysis as a thing-in-itself, and its particular manifestation in the patient's own experience of analysis, comes to form a link to the internal part-object—the maternal thinking breast as combined object, breast and nipple. The functions that the analyst is felt to perform within the analytical process assume definitive shape, greatly clarifying the nature of the felt dependence. Acting out in search of substitutes during the separation stands out clearly, showing either the adequacy or the inadequacy of these facsimiles. The analyst is therefore in a better position to help the patient to appraise the usefulness of these alternative relationships and not merely to oppose them on the assumption that they must necessarily impoverish the transference.

It is in this connection that the externalisation of the patient's narcissistic organisation with the individuals and groups comes under a new and more precise scrutiny, for the basis of judgement need not rest on value alone. It is true that shifting the basis of value judgement from moral or even ethical criteria to developmental ones (which often means suspension of judgement) softens the harshness of the analyst's interventions with regard to narcissistic-based relationships, since his attitude is bound to lack a basis in demonstrable evidence, except for dreams. But when the modes of thought and avenues of communication can also be brought under scrutiny it is often possible to demonstrate the deficits in quality of thought. This is most clear when a Basic Assumption Group involvement is at issue, but even in the ganging with one or more acquaintances the "misjoyning" functions of the Negative Grid (Milton's "mimic fansie" [*Paradise Lost*, V.110]) can often be demonstrated.

This avenue of enquiry into group communication processes is surely a Bionic addition to our equipment for investigating the workings of narcissism. Nowhere is it more clear than with perverse areas of the personality which so quietly drain the vitality of object relations. And here Bion's formulation of positive and negative emotional links sheds a brilliant light. "But am I not a part of this man's emotional life?" the perverse area seems to say, claiming a certain respectability and rightful share in the world of human intimacy. A dualistic theory of Life and Death, of Creative and Destructive drives, gives no definitive answer except a grudging "Yes, but you must be subservient, integrated for good and creative ends"—something the perverse aspect will smilingly accept, secretly triumphant. But when the perverse trends are recognised as anti-emotions, minus L, H and K, no ground need be yielded to them in compromise.

The concept of a Negative Grid and the recognition by Bion that knowledge of the truth is necessary for the construction of effective lies (lies to oneself as well as to others), has delivered a powerful tool into our hands for scrutinising the content and operations of cynical attacks on the truth. While I have never found the Grid useful for analytic contemplation, as Bion originally suggested, its format is wonderfully revealing of shifts of levels of abstraction and accompanying paradoxical statements. This leads on to greater skill in examining the defensive and evasive functions of ambiguous language usage as well as defects in logical operations, pseudo-quantifications, false equations and spurious similes.

Taken together these tools for minute scrutiny of processes of thought and communication place the analyst in a far stronger position than ever before in the struggle to wrest infantile structures from the domination or influence of destructive parts of the personality which organise the narcissistic or Basic Assumption groupings internally or in the outside world.

Finally we must examine the important matter of our private and corporate definition of psychoanalysis and its implications for our methods of work in the consulting-room. I do not mean to refer to the political aspects of the problem, such as defining psychoanalysis as what members of The Psycho-Analytical Society do, or five-times-per-week by definition, or extra-institutional and so forth. These local definitions ar fitted to local political problems and are not of scientific interest. The important problems are ones of private definition and public presentation to one's colleagues.

Essentially our private definition must rest on two piers: the method and the process it engenders. Almost everyone in the field would agree that the essence of the method is the scrutiny and description of the transference by way of internal examination of the countertransference. There is far less agreement, or need of agreement, about the nature of the therapeutic process generated by these operations. It is not unlikely that the process varies from analyst to analyst, perhaps from patient to patient, in essential ways. But all would agree that each analyst needs, eventually, to have formulated his own conception of the type or range of processes that he considers useful in an analysis that is progressing.

It is clear that he cannot use therapeutic criteria, either observed or reported. There is after all no need for analysts to claim any monopoly of therapeutic potency.

Having formed such a conception of type or range of process, the analyst should be in a position to be more flexible in meeting the demands of his patients with regard to frequency, duration of sessions, spacing, missing of sessions or periods of therapy, methods of payment, use of the couch, bringing or sending of written or graphic materials, interviews with relatives. Caution can replace rigidity of style and method when basic personal concepts of method and process have been established from experience with the particular patient and practice in general. Modifications in style and method introduced by the analyst should still be viewed with the greatest suspicion and avoided, probably, except for bona fide organised research. But a flexible response to a patient's requests, based on experience and firmness of concept, backed by careful scrutiny of the previous and ensuing material, can have a beneficial, humanising and encouraging effect. The consequences for the analyst are, however, far more important. Such an orientation obliges him to engage in continual careful scrutiny of the rationale of his procedures and thus to promote his own learning from experience.

Note

1 "These are the times that try men's souls: the summer soldier and the sunshine patriot will, in this crisis, shrink from the service of his country" (Tom Paine, *The Crisis*, published shortly after *Common Sense*, both 1776) [Ed.].

CHAPTER TEN

Aesthetic conflict

Introduction by Lennart Rambert

Meltzer had long recognized that patients in successful analysis, when approaching weaning, often had experiences of an aesthetic relation to the object—be it their partner, nature, or the analysis as such.

His experiences, especially from child-analysis and from studies of life *in utero*, and not least, his memory of experiencing his newly delivered grandchild looking into his mother's eyes, convinced him that the mind's first whole hearted launch into the outer world is to the mother-in-reverie. In the ensuing enchantment, links form between the epistemological drive for Knowledge and the Bionic vectors of Love and Hate, resulting in a strong—but the same time brittle—convergence of passionate feeling-thinking: an emotional experience, and food for thought.

This is the mould for all future aesthetic experiences, outer and inner, and is the most sought for relation to the object/outer world all through life. For in order to explore more deeply the nature of the creative process in psychoanalysis, especially the role of the internal objects—the thinking breast and the combined object—in creating an ego-ideal, he together with his stepdaughter, the psychoanalytically well informed writer and artist Meg Harris Williams, turned to poetry and literature. They wrote this book together, even if their thoughts are presented in separate chapters; and experiencing analysis resonates with the poet's relation to his Muse.

When the analysand has found a "good enough" way through the anxieties of the schizoparanoid and depressive positions, Meltzer proposes an additional step in analysis: to "take the leap in the dark" and in the *presence* (i.e. not in dreams only) of the analyst fully experience the ambivalent feelings and turmoil of the aesthetic conflict. In the ensuing trust in himself, hopefully *his own* thinking breast and his own combined object will come to the fore; and his Muse will reign.

With this book, and its follower *The Claustrum*, Meltzer takes a bold and truly transformative grip on Kleinian analysis on both metapsychological and clinical levels and lays the ground for a postKleinian tradition in which life, in all its growing complexity, is basically aesthetic in nature and psychoanalysis a dyadic work of art—unique and presentational in form.

Aesthetic conflict[i]

(1988)

Once one has taken on board Bion's description of "an emotional experience" as the primary developmental event, it becomes clear that his "empty" concepts of alpha-function and beta-elements make essentially, a distinction between symbol-formation and thought on the one hand and a computation using signs and simple modes of extrapolation from past experience and received ideas, on the other. The creation of idiosyncratic symbols as opposed to the manipulation of

---

i Selections from Chapter 2 of Meltzer & Williams, *The Apprehension of Beauty* (1988), pp. 14-19, 24-26, 27-29.

conventional signs, marks the watershed between growth of the personality and adaptation. The tension between the two is the essence of what Freud labelled as "resistance to enquiry". Bion's distinction between "learning from experience" and "learning about" the world is precise. It is likewise marked by the distinction we make between narcissistic forms of identification (projective and adhesive) which produce an immediate and somewhat delusory alteration in the sense of identity, and the introjective process by which our internal objects are modified, setting up gradients of aspiration for the growth of the self.

Our lives are greatly occupied by relationships which are not intimate. Rousseau's *Social Contract* well describes the way in which we move about the world, using the lubrication of manner and custom, of conformity and social invisibility to minimize the friction and thus the wear and tear on our psyche-soma. And it is probably in this area that the majority of psycho-somatic dislocations take place. The "hostages to fate" aspect of our posture towards the casual world of teeming humanity, where "everything threatens the head that I love", intimidates us beyond our wildest imaginings. We strive to create, through our apparent docility to the requirements of the community, a private space in which to enjoy the usufruct of our inheritance without "let or hindrance". These manoeuvres create the social armour which Wilhelm Reich described so wonderfully. But we are confronted with the problem of removing it when "at home" and donning it again in time to sally forth. We dread to send our little children naked into the world of the nursery and the school, and later, to see them swallowed up by the great combine harvester of the adolescent community.

Of the people who do not manage the enclosure of this space of privacy and intimacy, two distinct classes—at the antipodes of the body of the community—can be distinguished. The first of these, comprising the mentally and socially ill, are cut off from intimacy by the severity of their delusional ideas: either from living in states of projective identification, or from a gross failure of development of the personality, or from such perseverance in infantile modes of relationship that intimacy of an adult sort cannot develop. The second class are the artists, whose pained perception of the inhumanities daily in force about them, juxtaposed to a vision of the beauty of the world being vandalised by these primitive social processes, forbids them to squander the huge blocks of life-time required for adaptation. If lucky, they are spared by the community from total neglect or persecution, but at the expense of having their work appropriated and misused, ridiculed and imitated all at the same time. The recent vogue in literary criticism is a precise example of acting-out ambivalence and hostility towards the artists.[i] At best they are treated as members of the amusement industry.

The huge majority of caring parents, seeing all about them the misery of maladaptation, cannot help being primarily concerned, in their methods of upbringing, with armouring their children against the inhumanities inflicted on both the poorly adapted and on those whose naked sensitivity makes them vulnerable to the grossness of inconsiderate behaviour in casual and contractual relations. Similarly our schools cannot resist the pressure from parents and government alike to direct their efforts toward producing employable grown-ups. One must see the facts without seeming to pretend that any alternative is close at hand. We wish to prepare our children for the beauties of intimacy but our anxieties for their survival overcome our judgement so that we find ourselves joining in the training process, knowing quite well that it will dampen their thirst for knowledge and constrict their openness to the beauties to which they stand heir.

Although this process reaches its climax in the establishment of the so-called latency period, close observation of family life and of the mother-infant relationship reveals evidence of its early commencement. No event of adult life is so calculated to arouse our awe of the beauty and our wonder at the intricate workings of what we call Nature (since we hesitate nowadays to cite first causes) as the events of procreation. No flower or bird of gorgeous plumage imposes upon us the mystery of the aesthetic experience like the sight of a young mother with her baby at the breast. We enter such a nursery as we would a cathedral or the great forests of

---

[i] Referring to the various modes of linguistic behaviourism prevalent in literary criticism from the 1970's until recently.

the Pacific coast, noiselessly, bareheaded. Winnicott's stirring little radio talks of many years ago on "The Ordinary Devoted Mother and her Baby" could just as well have spoken of the "ordinary beautiful devoted mother and her ordinary beautiful baby". He was right to use that word "ordinary", with its overtones of regularity and custom, rather than the statistical "average". The aesthetic experience of the mother with her baby is ordinary, regular, customary, for it has millennia behind it, since man first saw the world "as" beautiful. And we know this goes back at least to the last glaciation.

Correspondingly it is only the limitations in our ability to identify with the baby that leaves him—in our thoughts – denuded of mentality. This ordinary beautiful baby does come trailing Wordsworthian clouds of glory in his openness to the apprehension of the world about him, if not he wisdom that can make him "father to the man" (although, to do Wordsworth justice, his "little philosopher" is five years, not five days, old ["The Immortality Ode"). Proto-aesthetic experiences can well be imagined to have commenced in utero: "rocked in the cradle of the deep" of his mother's graceful walk; lulled by the music of her voice set against the syncopation of his own heart-beat and hers; responding in dance like a little seal, playful as a puppy. But moments of anxiety, short of foetal distress, may also attack the foetus: maternal anxiety may also transmit itself through heart-beat, rigidity, trembling, jarring movements; perhaps a coital activity may be disturbing rather than enjoyable, perhaps again dependent on the quality of maternal emotion; maternal fatigue may transmit itself by loss of postural tone and graceless movement. Perhaps above all the foetus may feel his growth as the narrowing of his home in typical claustrophobic fashion and deduce that life exists beyond its familiar bounds, a shocking idea to a natural flat-earther. Imagination is a foraging impulse; it will find food for thought in the desert.

How, then, may the bombardment of colour, form and patterned sound of such augmented intensity as greets the newborn, impinge upon his mind? This we must ask the moment we consider that the baby's mind may already have begun its functions of imaginatively and thoughtfully exploring the world of its emotional interest. The great variety of demeanour and behaviour of the newborn is too obvious for anyone seeing them in the mass, as in an obstetrical department, to ignore; but of course this has always been ascribed to variation in constitution, or temperament, or differing degrees of foetal distress during birth, etc. The making of such ascriptions has neither descriptive nor explanatory power and merely dismisses the problem. Certainly it is no more speculative to say that babies experience the birth process and the first encounters with the world of intense sensa with differing attitudes, ranging from complete aversion to ecstatic wonder at the "brave new world". Two great allegories encompass these opposite poles of the birth experience: namely, Harold Pinter's *The Birthday Party*, and Shakespeare's *The Tempest*, each of which defines with great clarity the baby's relation to the placenta and its transformations. Our poet's kaleidoscope-collection cabinet inside the house is an attacked placental image, just as the three images of his next dream reveal the jealously attacked "magnificent breasts".[i] Bion's paper on "The Imaginary Twin" (*Second Thoughts*, 1970) pursues this same theme of the imagery of the placenta; but only in his last work, the trilogy *A Memoir of the Future*, does he discuss the implications of a pre-natal mental life, and the role that the cut-off pre-natal parts of the personality play in later psychopathology.

This type of imaginative conjecture cannot aspire to any status other than that of being credible; or at least as credible as such unimaginative formulations as "constitution", "heredity", or "just like his father was as a baby". At any rate for our purpose here, it is quite sufficient to establish credibility as a basis for interest in the wider speculation for which, however, we do have evidence that is more than merely suggestive. Since this wider speculation is the heart of the matter of this book, it needs a small preamble of its own in the context of the history of psychoanalytical ideas.

Although it may not have found its official statement until "The Ego and the Id", from at least the time of "Little Hans" Freud was

---

i Referring to previously described dreams of a patient who was a poet: the first *a cabinet full of phials and pieces of coloured glass*; the second consisting of three images (*hedgerows, squash court, boxes*) that suggested the "monstrosity" of his mother's breasts emerging from her clothes in order to feed his baby sister.

aware that mental pain and mental—that is, intrapsychic—conflict were absolutely bound together. Such was Freud's Darwinian bias towards action as the ultimate goal of mental functioning that varieties of mental pain, generally lumped together as "anxiety"— including even the grief of mourning—needed to be given a heuristic value as "signal" of some danger. I say even the grief of mourning, for his emphasis is upon this emotion as signal that hopes and aspirations connected with the lost one require to be relinquished in the "work" of mourning.

There is a subtle though immensely significant change in attitude towards mental pain in the work of Melanie Klein. Its more obvious item is the classification of mental pains into persecutory and depressive, but this represents an expansion and clarification of Freud rather than a fundamental change in attitude. It is true that her classification somehow carries the implication that persecutory pain is "bad" and depressive pain "good" because they have reference to regressive and progressive developmental trends respectively. But the more important alteration—growing out of her forward-looking, developmental orientation as compared to Freud's essentially backwards-looking, psychopathological interest —is her insistence that a certain level of mental pain, different though it is for different people, is essential for development of the personality. It is true that she assumed that the basic developmental schema was inbuilt, either by genetics, pre-history, social process or internal logic; but she saw clearly that an optimal level of anxiety favoured developmental conflict and its resolution, while both too much and too little of such pain favoured stagnation or regression.

[...]

It is my distinct impression that [the] poisoned atmosphere of institutionalised psychoanalysis has bred a certain shyness about speaking of love in the transference and countertransference, for fear of appearing sentimental or of colluding in the covert aggression of the erotic transference. The term "good" has come to mean little other than "gratifying", while "truth" has lost its intentional quality and has been replaced by "verisimilitude" or a purely technical meaning something akin to "accurate" or perhaps "similar" in its geometric sense. Of course there is always the danger of the sharp edge of psychoanalytic instruments being blunted by the rubbery qualities of Humanism (what Meg Harris Williams calls "Softhumanism")[i] and Sociological Relativism. The absence of the vocabulary of aesthetics in the literature of psychoanalysis—at least in its theoretical vocabulary—is nowhere more stunningly illustrated than in Melanie Klein's *Narrative of a Child Analysis*. The terse and even harsh language of her theories, and their preponderant concern with the phenomenology of the paranoid-schizoid position, stands in astonishing contrast to the emotional, and certainly at times passionate, climate of her relationship to Richard and of his overwhelming preoccupation with the vulnerability of the beauty of the world to Hitler's destructiveness and his own.

Thus it is that the literature of psychoanalysis, anxious for medical and scientific respectability, has also gone along unthinkingly with certain cultural preconceptions about babies. Everyone is agreed that mental life, in all its richness of emotionality, thought, judgement and decision, must start at some time. Systematic observation of the mother-infant relationship, as developed by Esther Bick and practised in the training of child psychotherapists at the Tavistock Clinic from as early as 1950, reveals unmistakeably the meaningfulness of what to casual observation seem to be the random patterns of the baby's activities. These early patterns, watched through their evolution in the first two years of life, tell a story of character development and lend emphasis to the importance of the matrix of relationship and communication between mother and infant from the very first moments of post-natal life. Similarly the impact of interferences such as prematurity, incubation, early separations, failure of breast feeding, physical illness in mother or baby reveal themselves in character development as unmistakeably as the "shakes" in a piece of timber mark early periods of drought.

It is necessary to plead for this recognition because the period of maximal beatification between mother and baby arises very early, soon to be clouded by varying degrees of post-partum depression

---

[i] A reference to M. H. Williams, "Knowing the mystery: against reductionism", (*Encounter* 67, 1986), pp. 48-53.

in the mother and, as I am asserting, the baby's reaction against the aesthetic impact. The picture of Madonna-and-child is not always very enduring, but it is deeply convincing. One can see its power repeated in later years when a grandmother holds her distressed grandchild, waiting for its mother to return to feed it; thirty years drop from her visage as the bliss of success in calming the child spreads through her being. It is this moment when the ordinary beautiful devoted mother holds her ordinary beautiful baby and they are lost in the aesthetic impact of one another that I wish to establish in all its power—and all its after-image of pain. "Isn't it a pity that they have to grow up!" What congruent shaft of pain goes through the baby?
[...]
The aesthetic conflict is different from the romantic agony in this respect: that its central experience of pain resides in uncertainty, tending towards distrust, verging on suspicion. The lover is naked as Othello to the whisperings of Iago, but is rescued by the quest for knowledge, the K-link, the desire to know rather than to possess the object of desire. The K-link points to the value of the desire as itself the stimulus to knowledge, not merely as a yearning for gratification and control over the object. Desire makes it possible, even essential, to give the object its freedom.

In my experience this is the heart of the essential shift manifest in the threshold phenomena between Ps and D. It is true, as Melanie Klein spelled out, that the shift involves the transformation from self-interest to safety and comfort to concern for the welfare of the loved object. But that does not describe the modus operandi of the shift. For in the interplay of joy and pain, engendering the love (L) and hate (H) links of ambivalence, it is the quest for understanding (K-link) that rescues the relationship from impasse. This is the point at which Negative Capability asserts itself, where Beauty and Truth meet.
[...]
There could well be countless babies who do not have ordinary devoted beautiful mothers who see them as ordinary beautiful babies, and who are not greeted by the dazzle of the sunrise. Yet I cannot claim with conviction that I have ever seen one in

my consulting room. Not even in my extensive experience of schizophrenic patients and psychotic children have I failed to find evidence of their having been touched by the beauty—and recoiled wildly from it, as they do again and again in the course of analysis. There is much evidence to suggest that being thus untouched is not compatible with survival, or at least with the survival of the mind.

As an addendum to existing theory this book is a piece of hindsight. I feel confident that in our consulting rooms, whether consciously or not, depending largely on the random factor of the training group and its particular chauvinist jargon, psychoanalysts in general—for at least the last thirty years—have been treating the phenomena which Melanie Klein labelled as paranoid-schizoid and depressive positions in the way I am describing. The psychopathology which we study and allege to treat has its primary basis in the flight from the pain of the aesthetic conflict. The impact of separation, of deprivation emotional and physical, of physical illness, of oedipal conflict pregenital and genital, of chance events, of seductions and brutality, of indulgence and over-protection, of family disintegration, of the death of parents or siblings—all these derive the core of their significance for the developmental process from their conribution as aspects of the underlying, fundamental process of avoidance of the impact of the beauty of the world, and of passionate intimacy with another human being. It is necessary for our understanding of our patients, for a sympathetic view of the hardness, coldness and brutality that repeatedly bursts through in the transference and countertransference, to recognize that conflict about the *present* object is prior in significance to the host of anxieties over the *absent* object.

CHAPTER ELEVEN

On Bion's Grid: later thoughts

Introduction by Robert Oelsner

In this talk Meltzer reappraises Bion's achievement in capturing something of the essence of the process of thinking through a Grid that parallels Mendelejeff's Periodic Table in chemistry,[1] making of both aesthetic objects.

Meltzer points out that in view of the evolution of Bion's later ideas and his own, the Grid needs some revision: one being that Myth formations (row C) seem nowadays to be a part of alpha-function (row B) rather than a distinct category. Mothers need to tell themselves little stories or private myths in order to establish a state of reverie with their infant: "the baby is hungry", "you need to sleep, sweetie", etc. Later more complex stories like the Oedipus myth, the myths of Eden, Babel, Ur and Palinurus cited by Bion capture essential aspects of the personality.

Another correction Bion had in mind, Meltzer reminds us, was Column 2 (lying), inserted oddly in the middle of the Grid, later to give way to the idea of an entire Negative Grid. Then, Action (Column 6) is the end of thinking, and could therefore be inserted in any column, with differing results. Action as a result of thinking has a different quality from acting-out, which precludes thinking. And finally, Meltzer suggests that Scientific Deductive System (Row G) and Algebraic Calculus—so far an empty category in the Grid, like Mendelejeff's then undiscovered chemical elements—should be replaced by aesthetic and spiritual values.

At the end of his talk Meltzer ties Bion's Grid with his late work *A Memoir of the Future* in which he tries to formulate his thoughts about the thinking process in poetical and science-fictional ways. It is a direct application of the circular or spiral progression of the Grid, where each ending of a cycle of thinking becomes source and inspiration for a new cycle.

The Grid[i]
(1995)

Having hated the Grid for years, I understand that most people hate the Grid, but I hope by the end of this evening you will love it. Once you wrestle with it, it's a thing of real beauty. It's based on another thing of great beauty in scientific history and that's the marvelous Periodic Table in chemistry. Like all works of art, the combination of form and function is really wedded in the Periodic Table and it's really wedded in the Grid. Behind it lies all Bion's theory of thinking and I will assume you know that well enough so I need hardly mention it.

The general principle behind the Grid and the thing that the Grid is trying to express, and to express really beautifully, is this idea that the mind does generate and develop thoughts; and that generating and developing thoughts is what we call thinking. In a certain sense, this is a reversal of the general attitude and philosophical statement that thinking generates thoughts. Bion's idea was that thoughts require an apparatus to think them. And that the thoughts themselves generate this apparatus for thinking

---

[i] From a talk by Meltzer given in Buenos Aires in 1995, transcribed by R. Oelsner. To be published in C. Mawson (Ed.) Bion Today (Routledge, 2010).

them, and thinking them means to develop them in abstraction, sophistication, complexity.

The fundamental thing in Bion's theory of thinking is that something transforms the observation of emotional states, transforms these observations into symbols. And if this function doesn't operate, the emotional states accumulate as accretions of stimuli that threaten to destroy the apparatus. Ordinarily, in the absence of symbol formation, what the mind has to do in order to cope with this accumulation of accretion of stimuli is to expel them. Bion identified a whole series of techniques that the mind can use to rid itself of these accretions of stimuli. He described them, and they all have great clinical importance.

The first technique is to reverse the functions of the special senses from taking in to expelling and to producing hallucinations. We call the clinical manifestations of this "transformations in hallucinosis". In more primitive states, the accretions of stimuli can be expelled or evacuated by meaningless actions, meaningless noises that have a similarity to language. That also has clinical significance in identifying a way of talking that he called the beta screen, a kind of talking that is meaningless but is capable of projecting great confusion, drowsiness, stupidity and so on. Perhaps, most important of all, that the evacuation of these unsymbolised accretions of stimuli can go directly into the innervations of the body and produce psychosomatic phenomena. That is Bion's theory of psychosomatic phenomena and psychosomatic illness.

This theory of psychosomatic illness brings these phenomena within the range of psychoanalytic treatment, but in a way that is quite different from that one might ordinarily think of for analyzing them. Because it says that what is required is an amplification of symbol formation. That's something that we are, in a way, accustomed to in the treatment of certain children whose symbol formation is very defective, who generally manifest what is known as the "hyperactivity syndrome".[2] And who respond rather marvellously to psychoanalytic therapy in a way that is based almost entirely on very primitive identifications with a therapist who keeps on talking, who is continually giving voice to observations and thoughts.

To get back to symbol formation and to the function that Bion rather puckishly labelled "alpha function". Bion's idea was that alpha function—that is, the original conversion of mental, emotional states into symbols in the mind—was a function performed by the mother for the baby. It is performed by what he calls the mother's reverie, which doesn't have to wait for the baby to be born, quite clearly, because the mother has states of reverie and states of communication with the fetus in the uterus.

And now with systematic studies on foetal life and foetal relationships going ahead, it begins to appear that personality development starts quite early in the uterus. Bion's idea was that the mother performs this function for the baby. She receives through the baby's behavior these states of confusion that the baby is in, and through her reverie and unconscious mental processes she puts some kind of order and sense into this chaos. She then somehow communicates and transmits this to the baby.

So, the mysterious process of introjection which enables the baby to establish an internal object very early, is of an object that can perform alpha function for it. This establishes the possibility of the baby being without immediate contact with the mother. And that, of course, is of tremendous importance for the baby's development: it is not like a little monkey that absolutely has to cling to its mother to stay alive.

Now the problem of the Grid, and its interest, starts at this point. What happens in the mind of the child or the adult once the symbols have been formed by this internal object that performs alpha function for him? Bion has drawn up this Periodic Table for the development of thinking and the evolution of thoughts. Although it is square, the processes that it depicts are essentially circular and spiralling.

That concept of the circulation and the movement of thoughts in the mind, that they move in circular ways through certain steps that are intrinsic and are required for the development of thoughts, is depicted by the horizontal and the vertical columns. The columns mark the progression of the circulating thoughts, their stages of evolution and complexity—abstraction, organization, generalization and so on. This horizontal axis and these vertical columns describe the mental actions that are taking place, through which the thoughts are being developed. This original form of the Grid has many defects in it, most of which Bion corrected himself in future publications. This progression through the beta elements, alpha elements, myths and so on, through preconceptions, scientific deductive systems and algebraic calculus, really requires some modification. Probably "myth" is in the wrong place.

Bion thought that alpha function was not an observable mental function. Its existence could be construed from its consequences but its workings were not observable. I don't think that was necessarily correct and I think that myth formations are part of the method by which alpha function operates. Myths are pieces of history which are subjected to various kinds of conversation and representation until they become symbols.

These last two categories—scientific deductive system and algebraic calculus—came at a time when Bion was having a kind of romance with mathematics, which he eventually called the "Alice in Wonderland" type of mathematics. Certainly in the three volumes of the Memoir of the Future, this has been corrected in a way that can be transposed back to the Grid: you can replace scientific deductive systems with aesthetic values and you can replace the algebraic calculus with spiritual values.

This Column 2 which he put in to account for lying was eventually taken out of it, and his idea became what he called the "Negative Grid".[i] That is, its lies were fashioned by a process that simulated and caricatured the processes of the Grid. Bion was very impressed with the talent for lying and how, in fashioning fashion lies, it was necessary to know the truth in order to produce caricatures of it. I think that idea was probably a result of his awareness of the techniques that were used in the formation of the Nazi movement or some aspect of the communist system—the aggression, and so on.

The other thing that requires modification is this final column called "action".[ii] Bion very quickly became aware that action was really the end of thinking—it put a stop to thought. And that action

---

[i] Meltzer is pointing at the Grid in the room he is lecturing in.
[ii] Meltzer is pointing at Column 6 of the Grid.

was possible at any point. It represented a kind of short-circuiting of thought, and he was in the habit of quoting a mathematician who said that the answer is the misfortune of the question.³

If we tentatively accept these modifications of the Grid and don't throw it away—as Bion himself more or less turned away, because I think he really couldn't see any use for it clinically...

[...]

I want to get down really to these last categories that Bion called algebraic calculus and scientific deductive systems and which I'm replacing with aesthetic and spiritual. In the last volume of the Memoir of the Future, the debate that takes place in this so-called committee is all about aesthetic and spiritual values. That volume is Bion's picture of the group interior to the functions of the mind, the group of the Self integrated as much as it can be integrated by communication with one another. It seems fairly apparent that this committee meets under the ethos of the internal objects. They are not present, they are not participating but the atmosphere is the atmosphere that they've created.

In order for the internal thought processes to achieve that level, in which spiritual and aesthetic values are at the forefront, it is necessary for the process to have had an evolution—a possibility which is demonstrated by the Grid. One of the virtues of the Grid is that at this level the developing thought becomes a preconception which can be developed into a conception and into a concept and this can be fed back as a preconception and the thing can be worked over and over again.

In Bion's thought, these are not new ideas. This is the process of developing thoughts to the highest levels of abstraction and generalization of which the Self is capable. The new ideas that produce the catastrophic changes that move the personality forward at sudden leaps, all come from the internal objects. And these internal objects are developing, just as we study the development of the ego. They develop by the constant process of introjection that we call education.

Now, it is probably true that most people are not able to undertake creative thought. Creative thought doesn't seem to mean new ideas. It seems to mean being able to develop the received ideas to these levels of aesthetic and spiritual values. Now, from this point of view science and art are completely indistinguishable and the great peril is in the area of implementation, of action. Of course, in our culture, one sees how this premature leap into action takes place long before its consequences can be discerned and always at the expense of something that is only later discovered to be the depletion of the resources of the planet, damaging the inhabitants, damaging the atmosphere of the planet and so on.

What I put before you in terms of Bion's philosophy is that action and the valuing of actions—what I would call military values—is still very, very dominant in the human race and needs to be opposed by inaction which is fundamentally, in the words of [Henry]David Thoreau [1849], the obligation to disobedience. Inaction isn't sufficient. What is required is disobedience. But clearly in order to be disobedient one has to think for oneself. And people are not very well equipped for doing that. But that I would think is certainly the aim of psychoanalysis. Personally, I think that the time has passed when psychoanalysis can be viewed as a therapy for mental disturbance and that it is becoming and has become an education in thinking for yourself.

Now, this disappointingly rambling kind of lecture certainly hasn't made the Grid beloved to you. But I would just like to say one final word about its beauty and the way in which form and function is united. It pictures a process in the mind moving in this wonderfully circular way but also capable of spiralling forward and also capable of feeding back into itself to enrich itself by re-thinking and re-thinking. It seems to me to be positively sculptural in its depiction of what goes on inside the head.

Notes [R.O.]

1. On March 6th 1869, Mendelejeff made a formal presentation to the Russian Chemical Society, entitled "The Dependence between the Properties of the Atomic Weights of the Elements", which described elements according to both weight and valence.

2. This is what often is diagnosed as ADHD and sadly treated with medication.

3. Maurice Blanchot, "La réponse est le malheur de la question", cited frequently by Bion.

CHAPTER TWELVE

Signs, symbols and allegory

Introduction by Grete Tangen Andersen, Morten Andersen, Trond Holm, Jon Morgan Stokkeland, Lilian Stokkeland, Eirik Tjessem

In this selection of extracts from some of his later papers and talks, Meltzer elaborates on the essential distinction between signs and symbols. This is perhaps a good place to start for new students of his work: it marks the difference between mind and mindlessness; mindlessness here signifying all the essential adaptational and conventional processes (the use of signs) which do not require the meaning-generating and symbol-forming mind.

This vital distinction has many different roots and ramifications. Among the sources that he mentions are Wittgenstein's linguistic philosophy, Cassirer and Langer on symbolic forms, and—of course—Bion's work. One of the many, and highly interconnected, implications is the difference between received (conventional) symbols and autonomous (original) symbols. What distinguishes the autonomous symbols is that they "are created in the mind of the speaker." It makes one wonder; how is it that simple and even conventional words uttered, suddenly become true and meaningful? To convey emotional meaning by language is "not just a matter of symbol, not just a matter of words; it is also a matter of the music". This leads on to the relation between "saying it" and "meaning it" (Wittgenstein, 1953)—being sincere—and to Bion's distinction between "learning from experience" and "learning about". Learning from experience rests upon symbol formation, which in its essence is an intuitive and mysterious process. It cannot be controlled or negotiated. This gives an answer to the question about what kind of science psychoanalysis is: an observational and descriptive science—it cannot explain and predict.

In many ways this is a *leitmotif* in Meltzer's writings, but perhaps most thoroughly elaborated in *Dream Life* and *Studies in Extended Metapsychology*. Meltzer's work on symbols and signs is, in our view, a major contribution to psychoanalytic theory. As he concisely expresses it: "I think what we have to do is make the most of the language that is available and to be as poetic and precise as we can".

On the cruelty of symbol formation[i]
(1995)

Bion has made it very clear to us that the essence of thinking is symbol formation....The thing about poetry, is that it captures something. I am thinking about the techniques for capturing wild birds. You set up a net and you set up a means of throwing this net suddenly. You attract these birds to the area that would be covered by the net when it's thrown and then when they're gathered you suddenly arrange for the net to be sprung and to cover the birds. That seems to me to be a good metaphor for the way symbols are formed and they way they work: that they capture these wild birds of meaning. If you want to say "oh,

---

[i] This paragraph is taken from a talk by Meltzer on "Thought Disorders" (1995), unpublished, supplied by R. Oelsner.

but there's something cruel in that", I'm inclined to agree that there's something cruel in the whole process of symbol formation. There is something cruel about the way in which it surrounds the emotional experiences and captures them.

Signs and symbols[i]
(1997)

My paper on "Sincerity" was inspired by reading the later work of Wittgenstein in linguistic philosophy. In the *Philosophical Investigations* [1953] he spends quite a long time discussing meaning, the difference between "saying it" and "meaning it". It drew my attention to the problem in analysis of both the analyst meaning which he says to his patient, and the patient meaning what he says to the analyst. In the course of investigating this problem I became aware that language is not a very disciplined way of "meaning it" because language is so conventional. This led me on to a clearer differentiation in linguistic structures between signs and symbols, which tend to be equated with one another in the work of people like Saussure and Lacan. The thing about signs is that they are just a way of pointing at things; they use words to point. They consist almost exclusively of the conventional naming of things and functions. In so far as people use signs in communicating with one another, they cannot "mean" anything, they are simply pointing to the world. Now symbols are entirely different and very mysterious, because they are utterly intuitive and are containers for emotional meaning. One would be inclined to say that when people do use symbols in communicating with one another they automatically "mean it".

But a difficulty arises because not all symbols are autonomous —that is, created in the mind of the speaker. Most of the symbols we use in our communication are conventional, received symbols —received from other people [...].

---
[i] Extracts from "Concerning signs and symbols", *British Journal of Psychotherapy* (1997), Vol. 14(2), pp. 175-81.

It is the dream that comes to the rescue of the patient, as it does for the poet. Our language is very rich in words for describing objects and functions, but very poor in words for describing emotions. The poet is very dependent on his dreams as the gold mine where he finds his autonomous symbols. He finds them in his dream life. The same with the patient: if he cannot remember his dreams he is in the position of feeling absolutely paralysed to convey his emotion to his analyst except by acting out or acting in the transference. His dreams come to the rescue of his incapacity for conscious symbol formation. The dream language begins to fashion a poetry of its own, that is special to that patient and that analyst in their particular and unique transference countertransference relationship.

While it is true that the analyst may introduce into the discourse with the patient certain amount of his own poetry—his own symbol formation—the discourse is largely (in so far as it is creative) of the patient's creation, through the symbol formation contained in his dream structures. One of the most important indicators of analytic progress, to my mind, is the progress in the nature of the patient's dreaming. The general development is from long anecdotal dreams to short condensed symbolic dreams [...].

One of the things Esther Bick taught us was that the meaning of baby and child behaviour is not obvious. It is a matter of interpretation, and interpretation is something that grows out of careful observation. The meaning of a baby's behaviour comes as an intuition to the observer that grows out of noticing what is happening to the baby. Now this lesson of Mrs Bick's is one which she herself learnt first in psychoanalysis, and I think to some extent from Melanie Klein. The lesson is that the activity of the analyst is not primarily interpretation; it is first of all observation and description. When a description of what is happening in the transference and counter-transference can be agreed upon by patient and analyst, then its meaning or interpretation may gradually become apparent to both of them.

This orientation leads to certain difficulties which have been very apparent in the psychoanalytic movement: in particular, that people like Melanie Klein and Esther Bick who rely on careful observation for generating intuitions, develop a capacity to know what they think and what they feel, and to know it with great certainty. The problem is, when you know with certainty what your intuition is and you put it into words, it sounds as though you are speaking with omniscience, with great certainty of being correct. People like Mrs Klein and Esther Bick were always accused of being arbitrary, of being omnipotent, of trying to force their opinions on everybody by the degree of certainty with which they expressed them. But this was not due to their conviction of being right. It was due to their sense of knowing precisely what they thought and felt about a particular situation. This means that when they "said" something they "meant" it, and when they meant it they meant it was not there for negotiation. The negotiation of meaning is the usual way that people come to think that they think alike. These rather fruitless peace processes that we see going on all over the world are negotiations where everybody is trying to find some way of compromising by overstating their demands and being happy to settle for half. Now that kind of negotiating is not possible when a person knows with clarity what they think and feel.

The next difficulty occurs when you complain to Mrs Klein or Mrs Bick: "But you said something different yesterday!" and they reply: "I changed my mind". How can anyone change their mind if they saw so clearly the day before? New evidence.

Symbol and allegory[i]
(2000)

I am going to talk about two wonderful dreams that illustrate some things that have exercised and fascinated me for some time. The first dream we call "Bottom's Dream" because like Bottom's dream in *A Midsummer Night's Dream* [IV.I. 99-217] it "hath no bottom"—it has material you could dig into and dig into and always come up with an interesting discovery, indeed

---

[i] Transcript of a talk on "Symbol and allegory" given in Florence in February 2000, unpublished.

electrifying. The patient, a middle-aged woman, began her account of the dream by saying "nations were on the move". I didn't know what she meant by that but was certainly alerted to something interesting, and she described it geographically:

> *There was a first level that seemed to be on a flat arid African plain. The masses of people moving on this plain seemed urgent, hurrying as much as they could, not quite like refugees carrying their belongings on their head, but obviously going somewhere.*
>
> *The second level, which seemed to be somehow behind her, was on the top of a high plateau and these people seemed particularly ragged and depressed, more like refugees from somewhere like Kosovo, dragging themselves forward. She felt there was something dangerous about them. She thought neither of these two groups – those on the arid plateau below, or on the equally arid table-mountain plateau above – were able to see the horizon; everything looked flat to them. They were in a sense flat-earthers, people to whom the earth seemed flat. (The implication was of course that we were all flat-earthers who would fall off at the end.)*
>
> *The group that she was with herself was on the verdant side of this plateau, rich in grassland with some trees. The people she was moving with were not indolent but leisurely; they didn't seem either to be in a hurry to get somewhere or in a hurry to leave some place—neither fleeing nor desirous to attain.*

Her association was that these different tiered levels seemed to have not only geographical but geological significance. It reminded her of the way in which geological shifts cause earthquakes and volcanic eruptions and so on—geological levels with catastrophic implications. She thought the implications of the two groups of people fleeing, and people pursuing some goal, were very sociological. The picture certainly reminded me of the situation that pertained in the Civil War in the United States when there were massive liberations of Negro slaves. Marching caravans were formed of freed slaves believing they were to cross the river Jordan and gain the Promised Land, as in the Biblical ideology captured in their famous songs. The tragedy was that that when these columns of slaves came to the river, they marched on, entered it and drowned. It was a bit like the lemmings, a kind of mass suicidal delusion leading them forward, and very different from the refugees on the plateau who were obviously fleeing from persecution and dread and were themselves felt to be dangerous and aggressive in their flight.

Now I thought myself that this was also a commentary on mental states: related for instance to Freud's dictum that neurotics suffer from recollections, always looking backward and thinking about what happened in the past, and bound by what he called the repetition compulsion to repeat the conflicts and anxieties of the past. What he didn't make so clear was that patients like Emmy von N., for example, were constantly peering into the future and were always saying "what if this" and "what if that". They suffered constantly from the imaginary dangers conjectured through their "what-if"ing. One meets a lot of both these states in clinical practice: people caught between "if only" about the past and "what if" about the future; and between these two levels of conjecture about the past and conjecture about the future, the present moment was somehow compressed and was not experienced as the reality. The reality was all past and future; the present was the evanescent moment which was just passing like the view from a rapidly moving train—flashing past, it couldn't be lived in.

This seems to me to be the essential structure of symbol formation—complex moving at many different levels. The movements along the arid African plain also reminded my patient of animals in search of waterholes. So there are references to many levels of ideation within this symbol of symbol formation —geographical, geological, animal, human, and probably some attempt at discovering the present, represented by the verdant level between the arid plain and the arid plateau. On this verdant level it was possible for people to live in some sort of peace and to see the horizon in a way that informed them the earth was not flat, but that they were living on an object moving in space, in a system that had its own laws, which could be discovered and have predictions made about it, measurements taken and so on. So the system touched on the very ancient science of astronomy and its relation astrology. Just as, as archaeology discovers one ancient civilization after another, it always seems to be discovered that they had astrological ideas and ways of measuring the movements of the sun, moon and stars—that is, an awareness that we live as part of a planetary system.

This idea of a planetary system is in many ways the origin of religion, and really is applicable to everything. It would appear to be a fairly universal method of organization for individuals, whatever the level of abstraction within their unit self: they organize themselves as planetary systems. And of course the human family is the planetary unit of human life: it is natural that children circle in a planetary way around the parents, as sun and moon of their particular planetary system. And should any one of the children leave this planetary system (as Martha Harris and I tried to describe in our model)[i] they fall outside the planetary pull of the parents into what Kierkegaard would have called "despair". The most despairing situation being of course the schizophrenic type of illness, in which individuals have floated away from the human race and seem to be engaged nowhere, doing nothing, having no experiences—a vacuum of mental events that invites the systematic formation of delusions as a substitute for the self-evident facts of the planetary system of the family.

Today, of course, there is much worrying that this planetary system of the family has fallen to pieces—that owing to the number of divorces children are thrown from one planetary system into another, with step-parents, or thrown onto the community from neglect and so on. This deterioration of the family is believed to be consequent to the deterioration of religious beliefs—what is called (after Nietzsche) the "death of God", the collapse of the Catholic church and the arising of a plethora of religious cults of one sort or another. It does seem to threaten chaos, and as Virginia [Ungar]

---

[i] Meltzer & Harris, "A Psychoanalytic Model of the Child-in-the-Family-in-the-Community" (1976), in Hahn 1994 (ed.) *Sincerity: Collected Papers of Donald Meltzer*. See extract in Chapter 4 of this book.

was describing in her paper, reminds us of what we assume to be the mental state of the baby either before or after birth. But it is probably unfounded really. We forget that the genetic structure of the baby is something that has been prepared over millions of years and is in no sense chaotic. The speed with which children adapt themselves and learn, is evidence of the degree to which development is programmed from limitless past generations. The developmental roots are there, inbuilt. Techniques of parental care, whether at the level of the family or of local or state government or other assumed parental situations, need to reflect the fact that these programmed developmental roots already exist. The function of parents is not to prescribe progress, but to assist the growth from these roots….

Now I'd like to leave this first dream, which came at the beginning of a week two weeks before a holiday break, and to present a dream from two weeks later, just two days before the break. The patient dreamed that

> *she was in a rather large, luxurious boat, some sort of pleasure cruiser, very elegantly built. She was looking at the flooring and particularly admired the fine wood, brass fittings and so on. She was in what seemed to be a lounge with tables and chairs and a bar—clearly a luxury cruise. She didn't remember whether there were other people there, but she thinks probably there were. She went out on deck and was surprised by what she found there. On the deck towards the prow of the boat, at the front, she found an elaborate flower garden—not the sort of thing you expect to find on an ocean cruiser. Then she walked round to the stern of the boat, and there discovered a churchyard with tombstones, which also surprised her.*

Her association to this dream was that this boat was very similar to a type of boat that is actually built in a boatyard by the canal near which she lives. One boat is built at a time, a sort of Rolls-Royce of nautical elegance. However this canal is only suitable for longboats, it is too narrow for these "Rolls-Royces", so that when one is finished it has to be lifted by crane several miles to the Grand Union Canal which is wide enough to float it down to the sea.

Combining these associations with her dream's description of an elegant holiday cruise style of boat, I came to think of this as a "ship of fools", a mediaeval construction which has been the subject of various novels (for instance, by Katherine Anne Porter [1962]). This elegant and luxurious interior leads to the flower garden in the prow of the ship but also to the tombstones in the churchyard at the stern of the ship. Clearly this is meant to be an allegory, of birth and life and death: you spend nine months in elegant comfort and luxury in the womb, then you are born to a relatively evanescent blossoming but inevitably head for the graveyard. It is a ship of fools because it mocks at human optimism; and the way in which optimism is mocked indicates that the planning and planting of this ship is all a matter of human ingenuity. Human ingenuity has set up this ship with its garden and its tombstones—like a surrealistic painting, with its surprises and paradoxes, where objects and shadows are dissociated from one another in a surprising way.

Consider now this dream in juxtaposition to the first dream. It seems to me (and I'd ask Meg to comment on this) that what we have here is a distinction between allegory and symbol. Allegory I take to consist of the rather ingenious substitution of known elements for what is mysterious and unknown; it is a kind of cheat because it pretends to bring the unknown within the sphere of the already-known (that life is folly…and so on). Symbol, on the other hand, is like Bottom's dream, full of mystery, and inexhaustible however much you dig into it, like the varied dimensions of the first dream which really do embrace the history of the world; its many levels are not just an ingenious emblem. A symbol carries with it the gift of humility; you know perfectly well you will never understand it completely.

CHAPTER THIRTEEN

Some personal statements by Donald Meltzer

On his analysis with Melanie Klein[i]

She was even in her 70's a handsome woman, fond of big hats and dressing well. She lived alone with a maid and a visiting secretary and her cat in a fair sized first floor flat in Hampstead, on a hill with views. With me, a patient, she was very formal but not cold, attentive and observing and talking quite a lot, always to the point and full of her observations. At time of collapse, catastrophe or misery she seemed very strong and fearless. I knew from public situations that she could be aggressive and contemptuous but she was neither with me in the sessions. She seemed immune to seduction or flattery but could be very ambiguous about personal feeling for the analysand. The result was that through years of analysis I never really felt that she liked me nor should. She played the piano and had a grand in the waiting room which it took me some years to see. Her cat occasionally came in to the consulting room which annoyed me. She was punctilious

---
[i] From a letter, unpublished.

about punctuality, about her bills and holiday dates. Her memory seemed remarkable to the end.

Invention and Discovery[i]

To get back to this serious business of invention and discovery, which takes us directly to the differentiation between talent and genius. Talent is one of these miracles which are thrillingly more and more apparent as I grow older. I was looking at a book of drawings by a five and a half year old autistic girl who drew horses better than Pietro della Francesca, better than Uccello, and how she could draw these horses was a miracle. They were full of muscle, full of vitality; yet she looked so lacking in vitality herself in the photograph. When I was younger I thought that talent was simply a matter of good teaching and hard work, and that if you persevered you would discover your talents. It took a long time to realise that it didn't work like that. I had good teachers and I worked hard, but nothing happened. What did happen seemed so trivial that it was hardly worth mentioning: I discovered that I was a good reader of dreams, which seems utterly trivial—except that they are marvellous and mysterious and alert you to the fact that the human mind is something about which we actually know nothing.

The discovery that there are children who never get born is a really important one—children who do not make the transition from dependence on the placenta to dependence on the breast, with the result that they have no access to the communications that Bion has spelled out in terms of maternal reverie and so on. I certainly think I have seen children who failed to get born. Some of them are the kind of children who are called hyperactive and manifest an absolute incapacity for symbol-formation, thought. But how it comes about I can't say.

---

[i] From a lecture transcript; published as "The role of projective identification in the formation of weltanschauung", in N. Field (ed.), *Ten Lectures on Psychotherapy and Spirituality* (2005), pp. 131-36.

About how it doesn't come about I could say something. I think I have discovered something about the creativity of small children, and how it is connected with their earliest experiences of defecation: with what an achievement and triumph it is for a small child to produce a firm stool, and how it is required that this achievement be recognised. And most mothers do automatically recognise this achievement. But they don't recognise, as it were, the mechanics of it. What does a child have to do or avoid doing in order to produce a well-formed stool, which also turns out to be a good-smelling stool? One discovers things like: the role of procrastination, in children being incontinent of faeces; where the urge to defecate is not so mandatory that you can't postpone it and postpone it until it is too late, and before you know it you have filled your pants. Not only filled your pants, but it stinks. What the child apparently has to discover is not only not to procrastinate, but its opposite—to be patient, and to wait until his organ s ready to produce a well-formed stool.

Now this brings us really, like Cupid's arrow, back to the problem of identification and, I suppose, to love. To produce a well-formed sweet-smelling stool is a gift of love. And to be unable to do it is a terrible torment for children. It makes me think about my own life experience and what lies behind the one talent that I have discovered in myself, that is the ability to read dreams, and how it came about as the result of falling in love with Melanie Klein and approaching her like an arrow from the bow, determined to have analysis with her. Not a matter of desire—a matter of life and death.

The dream landscape[i]

My own work has followed its clinical nose and in its writing it is not very imaginative. Only in my consulting room am I imaginative, and therefore work artistically rather than scientifically. The dream is my landscape.

---

[i] From a letter, unpublished.

On the thinking breast[i]

What strikes me about these two patients is their rejection of dependence. In the case of the woman patient it doesn't seem so evident that she is rejecting dependence; it appears more as if some sort of intolerance to separation is resulting in her trying to do it all herself. The first patient, the man, seems much more grandiose and arrogant in his independence. His dream of trying to kill his other self (standing for his big brother) by throwing lighted matches into his mouth, seems to capture something about his difficulty in understanding what it means to receive a new idea—someone to *give you* a new idea. His model for a relationship was always that an object has to be dependent on him and his marvellous little mouth that secretes saliva into the breast and enables it to learn the "fox trot" [*a sequence from the dream*]. This has clarified for me the nature of the problem of dependence.

The model of dependence which I think we have always assumed was the model of the baby's relationship to the mother and the breast and included also some role of the father of protecting this Madonna and child and so on. Whereas Bion has proposed this other function of the breast which is called "the thinking breast", that performs this alpha function and creates the symbols that make thinking possible. This is perhaps the heart of the matter of dependence. It isn't simply a matter of containment or protection or comfort or pleasure and so on. It's a question of an object that can perform this particular function, that creates the symbols for which dreaming and thinking can proceed. That is represented in the first patient's dream, in this very peculiar way of throwing lighted matches into the mouth of himself or another representation of himself, with the intention of killing himself.... It seems to me that that image really bears some thinking about. It's not just a pun on matching and the breast matching. There's something about the ignition and the sudden lighting up and so on. We are so sophisticated about fire that we really don't remember what a

---

i From a talk on "Thought disorders" (1995), transcribed by R. Oelsner, unpublished.

precious thing it is to be able to make fire. I suppose we have to go back to Greek mythology to remember about this gift from the gods. This seems to me the role of the analyst—to strike fire in the mind of his patient. It is something that we would all feel fundamentally incapable of doing. We can't even carry on an interesting dinner table conversation, to say nothing of striking fire into people's minds. No, if it weren't for the transference we would be absolutely helpless to assist our patients. It's the transference from these internal objects which enables us to seem to perform functions for the patient that are essential to the development of their thinking.

Religion and psychoanalysis[i]

The problem with which every theological and philosophical system has attempted to grapple has finally found its proper venue, psychic reality.[i] A new proof of the existence of God has evolved most unexpectedly through an essentially iconoclastic method which has at the same time fused the concept of God with that of individual mind, thus putting an end for all time to the possibility of religion as a social institution beyond the participation of the individual. God is dead in the outside world and brought to life within, but only, as we know, through mourning. It would be a good historical joke if it were to turn out that a Jew had carried the reformation to its logical end-point. The paradox remains that the best aspect of the mind is beyond self and the self must evolve in its relation to its internal objects through dependence, ripening to obedience, and ending as the acceptance of inspired independence. Under their aegis!

The beginning of revealed religion[ii]

This is an attempt to formulate a metapsychology of the neonate: its aloneness between feeds, ignorance of the mother's mentality,

---
[i] The following paragraph is taken from *Sexual States of Mind* (1973), p. 78.
[ii] From "A reverie of the baby's interior preoccupation", written for the Psychoanalytic Group of Barcelona, unpublished in English.

schooled only by the rhythm of her services, unable to form symbols and have meaningful dreams, bound to sensation, at best anecdotal in recollection, not even linear, on the verge of chaos. It is not surprising if it comes out sounding like Genesis. In the beginning was the feed. What we are relying on is the galvanizing of intelligence by attention to the polarity, for it is not in the beginning was the formless infinite, but the placenta as the primary feeding object. We might call this the experience of surprise and rewrite our genesis as a process starting with birth and panic relieved by surprise, not only surprise at finding the breast but surprise at an extraneous intelligence, the beginning of revealed religion. All the functions described are the fruits of identification with the extraneous intelligence. In the beginning object relations and identification are simultaneous.

The institutionalization of religion[i]

The psychoanalytic process is a natural process that has been discovered and developed, rather than a process that has been invented. This process, involving the use of the transference to enable people to re-experience their infantile conflicts and to have a new opportunity to work them through to better solutions, is nothing new in the world. To my mind, the history of psychoanalysis is, first of all, the history of family life through the centuries. It is also the history of religion through the centuries, because it seems to me that religion has always been the institutionalizing of this parental situation, through which adult people have attempted to cope with their internal situation and to work it over and over in relation to some object in the outside world representing parental figures, so as to try to preserve and if possible improve their internal relationships. Of course it is true that the history of religion is full of miscarriages of religion when religious teachings have been misappropriated and converted into institutions for repression and control of some sort or another, but these are absolutely alien to the religious teachings upon which they were founded.

Psychoanalysis is not a religion for the reason that, in contrast

---

[i] From "Conflicts within the analytic community", unpublished, no date, probably late 1960's.

to all the religions in history, it has finally located these objects correctly as being internal objects not external. However there is always a dangerous tendency in psychoanalysis to forget this and to move in the direction of converting psychoanalysis into an organization for thought control and tyranny.

The uses of idealization[i]

Even in their "badness" the idealized parents illustrate the goodness to which, unhampered by infantile projective identifications (of adolescent qualities), the internal objects can develop. The firm establishment of the compartmentalization would seem to be the precondition for the evolution of qualities of mind of these parental figures, extrapolating to the infinity of truthfulness, goodness and wisdom—to godhead.

On the principles of child psychotherapy training[ii]

In my long connection with this profession, before there was an association or even a profession, I have seen its small beginnings at the Tavistock under Mrs Bick and its blossoming under Martha Harris. With the wise counsel of her husband, Roland Harris, she framed and carried out a programme whose pedagogical principles were "enabling and inspiring".

These two principles have a multiplicity of consequences, both positive and negative. They are meant to encourage hard work, to support the student in difficulties, to encourage an *esprit* of friendly interest among students and with the staff. Just as important, these two principles are meant to discourage elitism, competitiveness and exhibitionism, to minimize obedience and persecutory anxieties.

Under Mattie's inspiring example the Tavistock course blossomed and became the model for the resurgence of child analysis in Europe and South America. The policy of virtual

---
[i] From *The Claustrum* (1992), p. 66.
[ii] From an open letter to the Association of Child Psychotherapists, 1992, unpublished.

non-selection of students, of a free hand to teahers and qualification upon completion of stringent requirements was manifestly successful. In the years following her retirement as senior tutor her functions were undertaken by a group of experienced people working under the pressure of an ever increasing demand for training. The tide of institutionalization started to creep in, led by its hallmark, committee-formation.

You will ask, "what is wrong with committees?" I will give you my honest opinion, based on experience. A committee, under the guise of democratic sharing of responsibility, becomes inevitably a cloak for irresponsible tyranny. That is the long and short of it. Where committees flourish, esprit leads to obedience, enthusiasm gives way to ambition, and truthfulness hides its head. Committees cheerfully take on functions for which enabling and inspiration have no place. It is done in the name of keeping up standards and the pursuit of respectability for the organization. Under this seductive cloak the individual member is invited to shelter. To shelter from what? From the inadequacies of your colleagues? Look to the quality of your own work. From persecution by the law courts or the legislators? Look to the ethics of your own work. For as surely as you sacrifice individual responsibility and shelter in the group identity you will be plagued by primitive persecutory anxieties that gaze timidly into the future and neglect the present tasks.

On the nature of supervision[i]

M.B.O.: Do you think that supervision is a super vision, or a very special vision of the patient?

D.M.: Well as you know, in the earlier days of psychoanalysis, the supervision was called "control", which was a terrible term—for the supervisor to be controlling the analyst; even at the beginning students didn't like being controlled. It is

---

[i] Extract from R. and M.B. Oelsner, interview with Meltzer "On the nature of supervision", *British Journal of Psychotherapy* (2005), Vol. 21(3), pp. 455-61.

super in the sense that the supervisor is supposed to have more experience than either the junior or the student; in the supervision almost all the supervisor has to offer is really the proof of his experience, because we are not operating a science in the sense of anything that can be mathematized or quantified. We are working with the quality of things, particularly the quality of emotion, and of course, we all have experiences of life.

In many ways, because of their experiences of life, older people are expected to be wiser than young people--which they generally are. Older analysts certainly have had experience of many more clinical situations and therefore are expected to have, and do have, richer powers of discriminating between one analytic situation and another; and this they contribute, or should contribute.

It is very much in the spirit of psychoanalysis that this is meant to be a feeding situation—and not force feeding, but a feeding situation in which what you have to offer is laid before the student or the supervisee for him to select what suits him. I think it must be left really to the richness and the power of your ideas about the clinical material to make it palatable to the person who is being supervised, and you must try to avoid any kind of imposition of your ideas. For this reason, it is very important to stick to the clinical material, and not to wander into theoretical situations. In my view, theoretical considerations are something that can be left to the classroom, the seminar and so on.

Now of course, in order to do that, the person who is coming to the supervisor has to bring carefully prepared material. And, as you do here, it is always best for it to be in a written form, as well as verbal, so that as a supervisor, you get this interplay of what you read and what you hear. Even in a foreign language, if I'm listening to French or Spanish or Italian, the music of the language and the music of the voice gives, together with the written translation, a very rich impression of the clinical situation.

It is also important for me to get a visual sense of what the patient looks like and how the patient behaves, so that I really can imaginatively participate in the analytic situation that is going on. If it is done that way, supervision is very enjoyable and doesn't have the stress of being the actual analyst. It isn't quite like being a general behind the lines, but it is imaginatively there, except that you don't carry the weight of the anxieties of the emotions which go directly to the therapist. You get a second—what would you call it—a second integral or derivative of the clinical situation.

This then leads on to another consideration—that it is largely up to the supervisor to be so non-threatening that patients can easily bring honest material. It is very very easy to doctor the material, to barber it like a haircut, to make the interpretations that you have offered seem correct and adequate. I often tell people that really they should try to present mainly the material and not so much their interpretations. Young people are very shy about their interpretations and feel threatened the moment they tell them to you. So certainly with students, I always encourage them just to present the material and let me think about it and imaginatively enter into the material, but not for me to be sitting in judgment in any sense of their interpretations.

Now of course, that is partly because I don't think interpretations are as important as they are traditionally held to be in psychoanalysis. I think the relationship between analyst and patient is contained not just in the words, but in the music as well. It is terribly important and there is nothing you can do about that except, as a supervisor, to try to sweeten the music a bit with your own music and I think it does work that way—that when you are seeing things in a kindly and humorous way, it gets into your voice and transmits itself to the patient and lightens the atmosphere. The atmosphere is terribly important; you cannot teach atmosphere. You can only demonstrate atmosphere.

So these are my ideas on supervision. You can see is not like a master class in music. It is more of a participation—more like playing in the orchestra; just contributing [...]. I think the music of the human language and human voice is very primal. The music of the mother comes through to the baby. The deepening of the transference is very dependent on this music and much less dependent on the intellectual insight that you can commmunicate by interpretation.

On counter-transference and "showing it"[i]

Counter-transference is everything in psychoanalysis. The historical idea that you must not communicate the counter-transference is an illusion. You are communicating it in the music of your voice all the time. You have to be a bit careful about your music, so that it doesn't become tyrannical, or too pedagogical, and so on. But there is no way of hiding the counter-transference. You can only modulate it to avoid excesses. It is absolutely what the patient hears: he hears the counter-transference. What he hears of the meaning through interpretation is quite secondary.

Showing the countertransference[ii]

One of the messages of the *Memoir of the Future*, in the third volume, is that the development of thought requires communication. It does not require things to be put into action to test them in reality. That brings us to the limits of thought and the limits of communication. It is probably true that there is a limit to communication, a limit to what can be said. But saying it isn't the only form of communication. There is also the possibility of showing it in a way that is not acting out, that is not an action. How does one differentiate between showing it and acting out or acting in the counter-transference for that matter? I think the answer to that is really in the intention that you discern within yourself concerning the showing.

This has to do with the counter-transference and how much of the counter-transference one shows one's patient as part of the communication process through which the thoughts are developed. I think the truth is that you show your counter-transference much more than you intend to and that a sensitive and intelligent patient does pick up your emotional state very accurately. And that it is

---
[i] From "On the nature of supervision", *op. cit.*
[ii] From a talk given in Buenos Aires in 1995, transcribed by R. Oelsner, unpublished.

part of the matrix that we call contact. The ancient ideal of the blank screen is just a myth, and not a desirable one.

These are things that one learns in child analysis, because in child analysis a great deal of showing goes on. In order to establish the analytic situation with children it is inevitable that you will show a great deal of your counter-transference. Simply keeping a child in the room requires a lot of showing of one's feelings.

On observation and counter-dreaming[i]

The first step is to recognise that the state of "observation" is essentially a resting state. Second, that it is also a state of heightened vigilance. I compare it with waiting in the dark for the deer, grazing at night, seen by their flashing white tails. This nocturnal vigilance is on the alert for movement of the quarry, part-object minimal movements which with patience can be seen to form a pattern of incipient meaning "cast before". This catching of the incipient meaning cast before is a function of receptive imagination, "open to the possible", unconcerned with probability. Being rich with suspense, it is necessarily fatiguing, even exhausting. However, it is a poetry generator.

Counter-dreaming

It is difficult to explain the technique of counter-dreaming. It is not enough to fall asleep while the patient is talking. It requires a process of working over the material, focussing and selecting interpretive configurations awaiting a state of satisfaction (rest). Remembering the material is essential, exhausting, fraught with anxiety. The opportunities of argumentativeness are rife and inviting, another area of fatigue for the analyst. It is all open to mockery … It amounts to the analyst having to "run a gamut" of persecution. Fatigue and irritation are the result, the trial of strength (and faith). This gives substance to a term like resistance or retreat.

---

[i] From notes contributed to M. H. Williams, *The Vale of Soulmaking* (2005), pp. 181-82.

Good luck[i]

With analysis, you always have to wait to find out what happens. Or did nothing happen? This is where the mystery lies: something rather mysterious happened, and it happened in this space created by the analyst and patient, in this mythological space of psychic reality. The patient discovers experiences he has never had before, and he tells the analyst that he has never had this experience before; and the analyst believes him because he wants to believe that something has happened, which is really not definable, but has happened in the Bionic space of the absence of memory and desire—more correctly called ignorance—which requires a kind of relaxation and trust in the analytical process as something that has a momentum of its own and finds a means of expression that goes beyond words.

[...]

Well that's it. The enemy is retreating – not from your wisdom but from their folly, from their having attempted to capture a frozen space and getting themselves frozen in the process. That's the kind of game you've been playing. Now the survival in this kind of game depends on what is called good luck. Good luck. And when you translate "good luck", it means, trust in your good objects. Good luck for the survival that you never could have planned, and that happened in spite of all your cleverness and ingenuity.

---

[i] From transcript of a talk given at a conference in Barcelona in 2002, published as "Good luck" in R. Castella, C. Tabbia & L. Farre (eds.), *Supervisions with Donald Meltzer* (2003), pp. 317-18.

MELTZER'S BOOKS AND CONCEPTS

Books by Donald Meltzer

1967 The Psychoanalytical Process
The process has a "natural history", starting with the gathering of the transference, then progresses through the sorting of geographical and of zonal confusions to the threshold of the depressive position, and is completed by the weaning process.

1971 Sincerity: a study in the atmosphere of human relations
Differentiates lies from the incapacity to "mean it" in the context of clinical material and three plays by Harold Pinter. (First published in Hahn [ed.], 1994)

1973 Sexual States of Mind
Sexuality manifests itself in childish, adult, or perverse states of mind, according to the unconscious underlying phantasy of the primal scene.

1975 Explorations in Autism (with John Bremner, Shirley Hoxter, Doreen Weddell, Isca Wittenberg)
Child cases supervised by Meltzer movingly demonstrate attempts to mitigate the intense emotional impact of objects in mental space.

Relevant not only to autism but to our understanding of psychic conflict in general.

1976 A psychoanalytical model of the child-in-the-family-in-the-community (with Martha Harris); in Hahn (ed.), 1994

Bion's "learning from experience" applied to family and educational situations, comprising an analysis of internal dimensionality and types of mental and social organization.

1978 The Kleinian Development (3 volumes: Freud's clinical development; Richard week-by-week; the clinical significance of the work of Bion)

Lectures on psychoanalytic history originally given to students at the Tavistock. Meltzer sees this line of thinking as inherently logical, but sees a split in Freud between theoretician and clinician. Klein adds a theological model; Bion an epistemological one.

1983 Dream Life: a re-examination of the psychoanalytical theory and technique

Dreams are not just puzzles to be decoded, the result of past trauma or wish-fulfilment, but the psyche's attempt to orient itself towards reality both internal and external.

1986 Studies in Extended Metapsychology: clinical applications of Bion's ideas

Emphasizes the essential distinction between thinking and non-thinking mentalities, in groups and within the individual. Discusses a variety of clinical cases by colleagues from early childhood on.

1988 The Apprehension of Beauty: the role of aesthetic conflict in development, art and violence (with Meg Harris Williams)

The aesthetic conflict originates at birth in response to the enigma of the mother's moods and actions. The book pursues the implications of the psychoanalytic process as aesthetic object (first mooted in *The Psychoanalytical Process*) and introduces a conception of psychoanalysis as an art form with analogies to literary criticism.

1992 The Claustrum: an investigation of claustrophobic phenomena

Instead of life and death instincts at work, Meltzer sees three distinct narcissistic worlds in relation to phantasies of living in a compartmentalised internal mother.

Some Meltzerian concepts

Pre-formed transference and gathering of the transference
Distinguishing the true transference (a present relationship) from the preconceptions brought by the analysand—can block communication or seduce the analyst. (*The Psychoanalytical Process*)

The toilet-breast
An essential function of the breast as earliest object. (*The Psychoanalytical Process*)

Projective and intrusive identification
Distinguishes communicative projective identification (essential to development) from pathological attempts to control the mother/object. (*Studies in Extended Metapsychology*)

Adhesive identification
Bick's concept illuminated by work with autistic children who "dismantle" their object; distinct from attacking or intruding into the object. (*Explorations in Autism*)

Aesthetic conflict
A concept drawn from poetry; seen as the key to mental development. Instead of innate life and death instincts is the tension between love and hate of the mother/object, beginning at birth. (*The Apprehension of Beauty*)

Combined object
Observed and formulated by Mrs Klein, who saw it as a rather dark, overwhelming concept; adapted by Meltzer in association with Bion's "catastrophic change" to represent a necessary and beneficial developmental force. (*The Kleinian Development*)

Sexuality
In accordance with Freud, the key to everything; but Meltzer differentiates perversity from psychosexual exploration, especially in the case of adolescents, and sees unconscious phantasy—not action—as the key to its meaning. (*Sexual States of Mind*)

The Claustrum
An expansion and elaboration of intrusive identification into three areas of the internal mother's body: genital, rectal and head-breast.

Pseudo-maturity
The result of living in the head-breast chamber of the Claustrum, intolerant of ignorance. (*The Claustrum*)

Tyranny
Sadomasochistic result of living in the rectal chamber of the Claustrum.

Dream-life and symbol formation
Meltzer's view of stages in thinking (enhanced by Bion's Grid) is founded firmly on Klein's drama of part-objects (mother's or father's body) acting as protagonists in a "theatre of phantasy". (*Dream Life* and *Studies in Extended Metapsychology*)

The countertransference dream
Meltzer's equivalent to Bion's "reverie"—the state of mind necessary for psychoanalytical work when it is a mutual communication, taking place in the present. It is based on mother-baby communication. (Meltzer, "Creativity and the countertransference", Chapter 8 in M.H. Williams, *The Vale of Soulmaking*)

REFERENCES

Bick, E. (1968). The experience of the skin in early object relations. *International Journal of Psycho-analysis*, 49: 484-86. Reprinted in M.H. Williams (Ed.), *Collected Papers of Martha Harris and Esther Bick* (pp. 114-120). Perthshire: Clunie Press, 1987.
Bion, W. R. (1962). *Learning from Experience*. London: Heinemann.
Bion, W. R. (1965) *Transformations*. London: Heinemann.
Bion, W. R. (1967). *Second Thoughts*. London: Heinemann.
Bion, W. R. (1970). *Attention and Interpretation*. London: Tavistock.
Bion, W. R. (1977). *Seven Servants*. New York: Aronson (reprints *Learning from Experience, Elements of Psycho-analysis, Transformations,* and *Attention and Interpretation*).
W.R. Bion (1991). *A Memoir of the Future* (first published 3 vols. 1975-79). Single volume edition London: Karnac.
Bronte, E. (1847). *Wuthering Heights*. Ed. D. Daiches. Harmondsworth: Penguin, 1965.
Breuer, J., & Freud, S. (1895). *Studies on Hysteria. S.E.*, 2.
Cassese, S. F. (2002). *An Introduction to the Work of Donald Meltzer*. London: Karnac.
Cassirer, E. (1923) *The Philosophy of Symbolic Forms*. Vol. 1: *Language*, trans. R. Manheim. New Haven: Yale University Press, 1955.

R. Castella, C. Tabbia, & L. Farre (Eds.). *Supervisions with Donald Meltzer.* London: Karnac, 2003.

Field, N. (Ed.). *Ten Lectures on Psychotherapy and Spirituality.* Karnac, 2005.

Freud, S. (1900). *The Interpretation of Dreams. S.E.,* 4-5. London: Hogarth.

Freud, S. (1911). Formulations on the two principles of mental functioning. *S.E.,* 12: 218-26. London: Hogarth.

Freud, S. (1917). Mourning and Melancholia. *S.E.,* 14: 239-58. London: Hogarth.

Freud, S. (1918). *From the history of an infantile neurosis. S.E.,* 17: 7-122. London: Hogarth.

Freud, S. (1923). *The Ego and the Id. S.E.,* 19: 3-66. London: Hogarth.

Glover, N. (2009). *Psychoanalytic Aesthetics.* London: Harris Meltzer Trust.

Gosso, S. (2004). *Psychoanalysis and Art: Kleinian Perspectives.* London: Karnac.

Hahn, A. (1994). (Ed.). *Sincerity: Collected papers of Donald Meltzer.* London: Karnac.

Harris, M. (1978). The individual in the group: on learning to work with the psycho-analytical method. In M. H. Williams (Ed.), *Collected Papers of Martha Harris and Esther Bick* (pp. 322-39). Perthshire: Clunie Press, 1987.

Isaacs, S. (1952) The nature and function of phantasy. In: J. Riviere (Ed.), *Developments in Psycho-analysis* (pp. 67-121). London: Hogarth.

Kierkegaard, S. (1941). *Fear and Trembling.* Princeton University Press.

Klein, M. (1932). *The Psycho-Analysis of Children.* London: Hogarth.

Klein, M. (1946). Notes on some schizoid mechanisms. In: M. Klein, P. Heimann, S. Isaacs & J. Riviere (Eds.), *Developments in Psycho-Analysis* (pp. 292-230). London: Hogarth, 1952.

Klein, M. (1957) *Envy and Gratitude.* London: Hogarth.

Klein, M. (1951). *Narrative of a Child Analysis.* London: Hogarth.

Langer, S. (1942). *Philosophy in a New Key.* Cambridge Mass: Harvard University Press.

Meltzer, D. (1967). *The Psycho-Analytical Process.* London: Heinemann. Reprinted: Harris Meltzer Trust, 2008.

Meltzer, D. (1973a). *Sexual States of Mind.* Perthshire: Clunie Press. Reprinted: Harris Meltzer Trust, 2008.

Meltzer, D. (1973b). Routine and inspired interpretations. In: A. Hahn (Ed.), 1994, pp. 290-306.
Meltzer, D. (1975). *Explorations in Autism*. Perthshire: Clunie Press. Reprinted: Harris Meltzer Trust, 2008.
Meltzer, D. (1976). Temperature and distance as technical dimensions of interpretation. In: A. Hahn (Ed.), 1994, pp. 374-86.
Meltzer, D. (1978). *The Kleinian Development*. 3 vols. Single-volume edition. Perthshire: Clunie Press. Reprinted: Harris Meltzer Trust, 2008.
Meltzer, D. (1981). Does Money-Kyrle's concept of "misconception" have any unique descriptive power? In: A. Hahn (Ed.), 1994, pp. 496-513.
Meltzer, D. (1983). *Dream Life*. Perthshire: Clunie Press. Reprinted: Harris Meltzer Trust, 2009.
Meltzer, D. (1986). *Studies in Extended Metapsychology: Clinical Applications of Bion's Ideas*. Perthshire: Clunie Press. Reprinted: Harris Meltzer Trust, 2008.
Meltzer, D. (1992). *The Claustrum*. Perthshire: Clunie Press. Reprinted: Harris Meltzer Trust, 2008.
Meltzer, D. (1995a). Thought disorders. Unpublished lecture. Ed. R. Oelsner.
Meltzer, D. (1995b). Talk on Bion's Grid. In press, in: C. Mawson (Ed.), *Bion Today*. London: Routledge, 2010.
Meltzer, D. (1997a). The evolution of object relations. *British Journal of Psychotherapy* 14(1): 60-66.
Meltzer, D. (1997b). Concerning signs and symbols. *British Journal of Psychotherapy* 14(2): 175-81.
Meltzer, D. (2003). Good Luck. In: R. Castella, C. Tabbia & L. Farre (2003), pp. 315-24. London: Karnac.
Meltzer, D. and Harris, M. (1976). A Psychoanalytical Model of the Child-in-the-Family-in-the-Community. In: A. Hahn (Ed.), 1994, pp. 387-54.
Meltzer, D. & Williams, M.H. (1988). *The Apprehension of Beauty: the Role of Aesthetic Conflict in Development, Art and Violence*. New edition: Harris Meltzer Trust, 2008.
Meltzer, D. & Stokes, A. (1963). Concerning the social basis of art. Reprinted in: D. Meltzer & M. H. Williams (1988), pp. 206-26.
Money-Kyrle, R. (1968). Cognitive Development. *International Journal of Psycho-analysis*, 49: 691-98. Reprinted in: D. Meltzer (Ed.),

Collected Papers of Roger Money-Kyrle (pp. 416-433). Perthshire: Clunie Press, 1978.

Paine, T. (1776). *The Crisis*. Reprinted in *Collected Writings of Thomas Paine*. New York: Classic House Books, 2009.

Phillips, H.B. (1960). (Ed.). *Felix Frankfurter Reminisces*. New York: Reynal.

Pinter, H. (1959). *The Birthday Party*. New York: Grove Press.

Porter, K. A. (1962). *Ship of Fools*. New York: Little Brown.

Rousseau, J. (1762). *The Social Contract*. Trans. M. Cranston. Harmondsworth: Penguin, 1968.

Segal, H. (1952). A psycho-analytical approach to aesthetics. *International Journal of Psycho-analysis*, 33: 196-207. Reprinted in S. Gosso (Ed.), 2004, pp. 42-61.

Sharpe, E. F. (1937). *Dream Analysis*. London: Hogarth Press.

Stokes, A. (1963). *Painting and the Inner World*. London: Tavistock.

Sullivan, H. S. (1953). *The interpersonal theory of psychiatry*. New York: Norton.

Thoreau, H. D. (1849). On the duty of civil disobedience. [Resistance to civil government.] In: E. Peabody (Ed.), *Aesthetic Papers* (pp. 189-213). Boston: The Editor.

Williams, M. H. (1986). Knowing the mystery: against reductionism. *Encounter*, 67 (June): 48-53.

Williams, M. H. (2005). *The Vale of Soulmaking: the Post-Kleinian Model of the Mind*. London: Karnac.

Wittgenstein, L. A. P. (1922). *Tractatus Logico-Philosophicus*. London: R and K Paul.

Wittgenstein, L. (1953). *Philosophical Investigations*. Oxford: Blackwell.

INDEX

Abraham, K. xii, 55, 69
acting in the transference 25, 27
adhesive identification xii, 19, 22, 35, 37, 81-5, 93, 105, 147
adolescence 36, 105, 137, 148
adult organization/part of self 9, 16, 28, 29, 30, 31, 32, 33, 40, 63, 105, 145
aesthetic
    conflict xii, 95, 97, 103-112, 146, 147
    object 90, 95-98, 104, 111-12, 113, 146, 147
    process in psychoanalysis 90, 92, 98
    proto-aesthetic experience 107
    reciprocity 22, 96
    relation to world 19, 58, 64, 92, 96
    values in Bion's Grid 113, 114, 117, 119
    vocabulary 110

aggression 30, 32, 48, 67, 73, 83, 117, 127, 131
alpha function 10, 15, 90, 94, 95, 96, 113, 117, 134
    and symbol formation 104, 116
analyst 2-5, 23, 49, 98
    as container 97, 143
    as dreamer 14
    as mother/father 48, 50, 60, 63, 75, 98
    flexibility 101
    patient's identification 8, 24,
    non-judgemental attitude 46
    role in society 70, 71, 77, 80
    self-defence 2, 3
    self-reflection 21, 49
    striking fire 135
    struggle of 22, 24, 26, 27, 62, 90, 100, 142
    as supervisor 3, 46, 138-40
    and symbolic language 124

analytic method
  emotional atmosphere 25
  exploratory 8, 23, 33
  reconstructive 11
  as thing-in-itself 87
  "translation" 13
anxiety 11, 21, 95
  the analyst's 142
  depressive/persecutory 28, 36, 38, 40, 74, 76, 77, 80, 82
  Klein/Freud view of 109
  maternal and the foetus 107
autistic children 19, 81-82, 93, 94, 132, 147
  and aesthetic sensibility 92, 97

baby/infant
  as aesthetic object 96, 111
  and breast 13, 63, 64,
  baby-part 41, 48, 65, 66
  baby-talk 31, 32, 33
  before birth 86, 103, 108, 129
  "inside babies" 19
  and maternal reverie 116, 148
  and mother 55, 85, 93, 106, 107, 113, 134, 140
  new baby 60, 67, 74
  observation in analytic training 110, 124
  and religion 139-40
basic assumption (Bion) 42, 43, 99, 100
Berkeley, G. 76
beta elements/screen 104, 115, 117
Bick, E.
  and adhesive identification 82, 93, 147
  and child psychotherapy training xi, 110, 124, 137
  psychic skin 84, 85. 86
  way of thinking 125

Bion, W. xiv, 1, 7, 14, 16, 28, 41, 56, 71, 89-101, 113-20, 122, 143
  Attention and Interpretation 43
  Learning from Experience 37
  Memoir of the Future 18, 114
  theory of thinking 10, 38, 47, 51, 52, 94, 115, 122, 134
  Second Thoughts 108
  Transformations 91, 92
body-ego 48
breast 33, 74, 78, 85
  as aesthetic object 92
  and baby 13, 48, 63, 64, 106, 110, 132, 136
  head-breast 56, 148
  representation of 10, 17, 61, 65, 67, 108
  and thinking 98, 104, 134
  toilet-breast/mummy 63, 147
Brecht, B. 16
Breuer, J. 57
Brown, R. 77

Cassese, S. F. xiii
Cassirer, E. 12, 121
catastrophic change (Bion) 92, 147
child analysis 137
combined object 40, 41, 63, 98, 104, 147
commensal/symbiotic (Bion) 43
community
  child and family 35-43
  psychoanalytic 91
container/contained 10, 83, 84, 89, 97, 123
countertransference 2, 14, 49, 56, 67, 97, 98, 100, 109, 112, 118, 124, 141
  acting in 3, 27, 34
  dream 22, 142, 148

creativity 4, 9, 33, 55, 59, 68, 73, 90, 124, 148
  and defaecation 133
  and drives 99
  of internal parents 41, 77-78
  psychoanalytic 103
curiosity
  epistemophilic instinct (Klein) 58, 67, 87, 93
  intrusive 38, 93

death instinct (Freud) xiii, 50, 51, 96, 99, 146, 147
defence mechanisms 15, 17, 67, 73, 75, 81, 93
delusion 47, 73, 74, 75, 77, 105, 127, 128
  of clarity of insight 55-68
  delusional learning 35
  delusional systems 16, 17
dependence 24, 59, 64, 71, 78, 98, 132, 134, 135
depressive position 5, 28, 40, 51, 70, 71, 73, 75, 78, 79, 93, 97, 145
  pain 75-80
  and weaning 2
dimensionality 19, 81, 82-84, 92-95, 146
  and alpha-function 95
dismantling of senses in autism xii, 81-82, 92-94, 147
dream(s) 9-10, 19, 32, 59-60, 63-65, 76, 108, 126-27, 129, 134
  as evidence 98-99
  flashes 12
  landscape 133
  as a language 13
  and thinking 7, 8
  theory of 7-19, 57
  see also countertransference dream

ego-strength 86, 96
emotional experiences 9, 10, 11, 15, 17, 62, 81, 87, 93, 103, 104
  and alpha-function 115-16
  anti-emotion 94, 99
  atmosphere 25-27, 40, 110, 140
  and empathy 52
  and language 122-24
  and learning 37
  mourning 109
envy 15, 48, 51, 58, 60, 78, 95

family 50, 106, 112, 128, 129, 136
  and community 35, 36-43
  human 76
  internal 10
Fenichel, O. 71-72
Frankfurter, F. 71
Freud, S. xii, xiii, xiv, 2, 3, 5, 23, 27, 33, 36, 47, 50, 51, 52, 69, 84, 87, 98, 127
  Dora 12, 27
  and dreams 7, 8, 11-14, 17, 18, 57
  ego and id 39, 50, 108
  "Little Hans" 109
  "Mourning and Melancholia" 18, 109
  "Rat Man" 86
  on resistance to enquiry 105
  Schreber case 19
  superego 40

geography of mental life 16, 52, 56
geometry, mental 48, 51
Glover, N. xiii
Gombrich, Ernst xiii
Gosso, Sandra xiii

Grid (Bion's) 10, 11, 15, 48, 90, 94, 99, 113-20, 148
growth of the mind 5, 8, 19, 34, 35, 42, 81, 105, 107

Harris, M. xi, xiv, 35, 37, 38, 89, 128, 137
Harris, R. xiv
hyperactive children 115

Imago Group xiii, 70
infantile feelings 15, 18, 136, 137
    development 39
    sexuality 69
    transference 12
    see also personality, infantile levels
inner world 25, 50, 57, 75, 76, 77, 87, 103
instinct, duality of (Freud) 47, 95, 96, 99, 146
    epistemophilic instinct (Klein) 58, 67, 87, 93
integration 5, 40, 41, 75, 85, 112
interpretation, psychoanalytic 21, 22, 28, 60, 61, 64, 75, 77
    correctness of 97, 140
    and material 58, 82, 98
    as metapsychological statement 23-24
    and observation 124
    music of 23, 57, 141
introjective identification 16, 40, 58, 81, 105
intrusive identification xii, 1, 38, 56, 85, 89, 93, 147
Isaacs, S. 11

Keats, J. 96
Kierkegaard, S. 68, 128
Klein, M. xii, xiii, xiv, 5, 24, 58, 64, 67, 81, 87, 93, 125, 131-32, 147
    on denial of psychic reality 17
    developments from 97, 104, 111, 124
    extension of Freud 7, 16, 18, 23, 36, 47, 52, 69, 90, 93, 95, 109
    and inner world 50
    and interior of mother 93
    Narrative of a Child Analysis 110
    "Notes on some Schizoid Mechanisms" 47, 52, 55, 112
    the positions, *see* depressive position
    and projective identification 1, 58
    on splitting 55, 66, 82, 84-85, 86
    and unconscious phantasy (Isaacs) xiii, 11-12
Kohut, H. 91

Langer, S. 12, 25, 121
language 43, 53, 57, 64, 89, 91, 97, 100, 115, 122-24
    of dreams 12-22
    of interpretation 24-25, 29
    of Klein's theories 110
    music of 139, 140
learning processes
    from experience (Bion) 37, 40, 58, 101, 105, 122, 146
    model of 35-43
L, H, K (Bion) 87, 99, 103, 111
    negative links 99-100
lies 10-11, 15, 17, 51-52, 89, 94, 100, 117
    see also Grid (Bion's)

masturbation 55-56, 73, 78
meaning 92-93, 110
    of baby's behaviour 124

INDEX 157

generated by dreams 7-19, 50, 57, 121-22
and language 64, 123, 125, 141
meaningless 115
misconception (Money-Kyrle) 52
and psychic reality 57, 79, 83, 85, 142
Meltzer, D., writings
The Apprehension of Beauty 22, 77, 82, 90, 104-12, 146, 147
"The apprehension of beauty" 95
"On Bion's Grid" 113-20
The Claustrum 56-68, 70, 104, 137, 146, 147
"Concerning signs and symbols" 123-25
"Concerning the social basis of art" 77
Dream Life 7-20, 56, 122, 146, 148
Explorations in Autism 56, 81-88, 92, 145, 147
"Good luck" 143
The Kleinian Development 7, 89, 90, 146
"A psychoanalytical model of the child" 15-44
The Psychoanalytical Process 2-6, 63, 145, 146, 147
"Temperature and distance" 21-34
"Thought disorders" 122-23
Sexual States of Mind 69-80, 135, 145,
Studies in Extended Metapsychology 56, 89-102, 122, 146, 147, 148
memory 48, 56
and desire (Bion) 13, 143

Mrs Klein's 132
Mendelejeff, D. I. 113
Milner, M. xiii
Milton, J. 86, 99
mindlessness 81-83, 121
Money-Kyrle, R. xiii, 39, 87
concept of misconception 45-53
mother 33, 62, 63, 64, 65, 66, 96, 103, 106, 113, 133, 134
analytic 29, 48, 50, 75,
breast 17, 78, 85
depression of 49, 85, 110
interior of 1, 16, 40, 55, 61, 79-80, 93,
internal 2, 56, 67, 74,
ordinary 82, 107, 111
and religion 135
as world 87
see also baby
see also reverie, maternal
myth 11, 43, 113, 117, 135, 142, 143

narcissistic identification/organization 16, 23, 34, 51, 55, 56, 58, 67, 78, 82, 84, 85, 99, 100, 105, 146
negative capability (Keats) 111

object (internal) 16, 19, 38, 52, 60, 66, 76, 78, 86, 87, 103, 104, 111, 147
absent 96, 112
aesthetic 92, 95, 97, 113, 146
bidimensional 81, 93
combined 41, 98
damaged 74-79, 85
introjection/ projection 24, 37, 55, 56, 59, 67, 105
organization of 39, 119
part-object 98, 142, 148

object *(continued)*
  qualities of 31, 38, 40, 42, 51, 71, 73, 82-85, 90, 93, 143
  thinking 116, 135
  (*see also* thinking breast)
object relations 5, 99, 136-37,
observation 30, 59, 73, 94, 95, 106, 110, 115, 124, 125, 131
  and counter-dreaming 142
  observational science 122
  of technique 34, 49, 57
Oedipal conflict 47, 59, 78, 112
omnipotence 41, 73, 74, 78, 83

pain, mental 11, 15, 17, 19, 28, 31, 47, 56, 66, 81, 95, 96
  of aesthetic conflict 111-12
  of depressive position 70, 73, 75-79, 109
  and learning from experience 36, 41
  from loss of control 33
  and pleasure 90
  and time 83
  of truth 52
Paine, T. 101
paranoid-schizoid position 1, 38, 104, 110, 112
persecutor/persecution 31, 36, 48, 69, 70, 77, 78, 79, 106, 127
  and absent object (Bion) 96
persecutory anxiety 28, 38, 85, 95, 109, 137-38
personality structure 14, 24, 25, 26, 37, 42, 47, 75, 87, 90, 105
  adult part 16, 28, 63
  conditions for growth 109, 119
  destructive/perverse 99, 100
  infantile levels 5, 10, 11, 28, 40, 41, 42, 50, 63, 64, 71, 78, 100
  pre-natal parts 108
Pinter, H. 17, 108, 145
placenta 108, 132, 136
Plato 15, 50
pleasure
  and comfort 134
  in Freud's theory 50
  and pain 90
poetic diction (Sharpe) 14, 122
  function 25
Porter, K. A. 130
projective identification (Klein) 1, 16, 25, 48, 52, 59, 83, 137
  communicative 89
  with internal objects 55, 60, 67
  as mode of learning 35, 37
  narcissistic/intrusive 58, 105, 147
psychic reality 57, 77, 79, 90, 93, 135, 143
  denial of (Klein) 17, 41
  and external reality 7, 17, 25, 48, 51, 56, 57, 72, 79, 137, 146
psychoanalytic process 1-2, 8, 17, 18, 24, 26, 74, 87, 103
  evolution of 89-90, 98, 118-20, 136, 143
  and method 23, 100-101
  and training 106

religion 128, 135-37
reparation (Klein) 75
reverie, maternal (Bion) 48, 49, 103, 116, 132, 135, 148
resistance 23, 64, 83
  to enquiry (Freud) 105
  analyst's own 142
Rousseau, J-J. 105

INDEX

sadism 40, 55, 60-61, 74, 85, 93
schizophrenic 66. 112, 128
Segal, H. 95
Shakespeare, W. 15, 56, 96, 108, 111
Sharpe, E. F. 14
skin as container (Bick) 82, 84, 85
sleep 10-12, 17, 19, 30, 31, 33, 78, 142
space, mental/psychic 16, 17, 47, 81, 83, 96, 143
spiritual values 117, 119
splitting processes 16, 25, 41, 52, 66, 71, 75, 81-87, 93
Stokes, A. xiii, 92, 77
Sullivan, H. S. 94
superego 40
symbol 12, 13, 72, 134
    and allegory 125-30and
    dream 8
    formation 89, 96, 104, 115-17, 122, 124, 132, 136, 148
    and signs 121-22, 123

temperature of communication 25, 27
terror of dead objects 69, 70, 7-80
theatre for generating meaning 7-19, 50, 148
time, oscillatory 83
thinking 36, 70,
    and action 114, 117
    breast 134
    and dream 7
    and internal objects 135
    and symbol-formation 8
    theory of (Bion) 10, 47, 51, 89, 94, 98, 103-4, 115-17, 120
Thoreau, H. D. 119
transference 4, 12, 22, 25, 42, 50, 67, 78, 99, 136, 140, 145
    acting in 25-27, 34, 124
    adult 40
    erotic 63, 109
    from internal objects 135
    perversion of 70
    preformed xii, 2, 147
    see also countertransference
truth/truthfulness 40, 52, 64, 66, 109, 111, 137, 138
    and lies 11, 15, 17, 51, 94, 100, 117
    as mental food 10

unconscious 2, 24, 27, 43, 47, 56, 80, 116
    and consciousness 4
    phantasy 1, 8, 11, 37, 67, 75, 77, 145, 147

verbal thought/ verbalization 12, 23, 24, 41, 48, 98, 139
weaning in psychoanalysis 2, 103, 145
wild analysis 27
Williams, M. H. 56, 110
Winnicott, D. W. 107
Wittgenstein, L.A.P. 12, 13, 25, 57, 64, 94, 121, 122, 123
Wollheim, R. xiii
Wordsworth, W. 95, 107
work-group (Bion) 41